The
MAKING
OF A
NEW
NIGERIA

**(Solutions to Corruption and
Underdevelopment)**

i |
(Solutions to Corruption and Underdevelopment)

OKORIE NDUBUISI SIMON

NERDC Recommended

The MAKING OF A NEW NIGERIA
(Solutions to Corruption and Underdevelopment)

OKORIE NDUBUISI SIMON

^^^

Okoriendubuisis@yahoo.com
08030759945

2nd EDITION
NERDC Recommended

Printed in USA by CreateSpace
ISBN-13: 978-1517068745

Remarks

The book, "The Making of a New Nigeria"is a necessary and timely addition to the corpus of literatures available on Nigeria as an energizing force in diverse areas in the world. Part of the uniqueness of the book is in the author's exhortatory style deploying facts at his disposal in galvanizing Nigerian's from all walks of life to be creative, innovative, and original. Indeed Okorie, a young and restless, budding intellectual and patriot, underscores the point that Nigeria may not reach its promised land in good time in its history if the people's mindsets are not changed for the better. He therefore deplores consummation as the base of Nigerian society, even as he articulates clearly the view that creative mindset in the people will greatly propel the nation to a higher height in its exploit among the committee of nations. His effort in this work is commendable, and will certainly have positive effects on the government

∧∧∧

TRANSFORMATION   AGENDA.   I
strongly recommend it to all.
Dr. John Otu

The book, the Making of a New
Nigeria: 'A solution to corruption and under
– development', is the result of one young
man's observation, study, research and
analysis of the social, economic,
technological and moral situation in Nigeria.
Mr. Ndubuisi Okorie evaluates Nigeria from
her birth and assesses her great potentials
then with the rich human and natural
resources she was endowed with even at that
early stage. He then highlights the present
level of economic downturn, technological
underdevelopment, political quagmire and
moral decadence in the country. He argues
that two major causes of the problem are the
value system of the people and their mind –
set. He concludes by proffering solutions
such as technology transfer, encouragement
and development of talent, emphasis on
education and moral development etc. A
study of this booklet reveals steps and
nuggets of wisdom and information and
ideas which if imbibed and implemented are
most likely to lead to an all-round

development of individuals, states and the country at large. It is recommended for all those interested in a better Nigeria.
Prof (Mrs) Ako Essien – Eyo,
University of Calabar.

In an era where morality and cultural norms are being relegated behind, a concerted effort is required by individuals, groups and corporate bodies to re-enthrone social order. Such social order is what is required for the overall wellbeing of a nation like Nigeria.

The development of any nation cannot be guaranteed if its citizens do not imbibe patriotic spirit as embodied in the doctrine of Positive Attitude. This is because, attitude is everything.

THE MAKING OF A NEW NIGERIA is an attempt in a right direction. The book is indeed a revelation of various hidden solutions to the socio – economic growth of our country, Nigeria.

I am particularly delighted by the author's effort in chapter four, to alert the public on the need for Nigeria to invest in talent harvest as wheel of our economic growth. If the popular saying that idea rules the world

ᴧᴧᴧ

is true, then what the author campaigns for here is that various talents hidden in Nigerians should be harnessed and properly put in use. The idea of pulling a round peg in a square hole should be de – emphasized in the running of Nigeria affairs.

There is no doubt that the book will be of great treasure to both students of social sciences at all level as well as the public. I therefore congratulate the author for this wonderful effort.

K. M. Mbam
Director,
Public Enlightenment,
Directorate of Attitudinal Change
Ebonyi State.

Dedication
This edition is dedicated to all who desire a
better Nigeria

∧∧∧

Acknowledgement

I give glory to God Almighty for the inspiration to write this intellectual masterpiece.

I acknowledge every individual, organizations and institutions which support projects that re - inform, transform and change the mindset of people positively.

A better Nigeria is formed when we harnessed our potentialities.

CONTENTS

^^^

^^^

FOREWORD

Nigeria Golden Jubilee has been aptly celebrated with hope and pride in the giant strides that the nation has made after 50 years of independence. Certainly, we Nigerians are indeed proud of the quantum leaps in the educational, economic, political, socio – cultural and aesthetic spheres.

Yet, Mr. Okorie Ndubuisi has cautioned our wholesale celebration in The Making of a New Nigeria, he has pointed out lapses in our value system and mindset as grey areas that must still be addressed more poignantly if Nigeria will actualize her apogee of development.

He has carefully crafted relevant chapters to convey his thoughts and pragmatic methods of realizing a holistic development in the years ahead. Perhaps, Okorie Ndubuisi has sounded a wake – up call which needs to be taken seriously by policy – makers and sundry.

I strongly recommend this volume for all Nigerians who look forward to a more fruitful celebration of her centenary.

Prof. Daniel I. Denga
Professor of Education
University of Calabar.

Preface

Nigeria is a multinational country. When compared with nations like Wales, it may not be far to call her United Nations or United States of Nigeria. Unlike the United States of America, Nigeria is a country of more than 250 ethnic groups with over 500 indigenous languages. The country is not just a nation but the amalgamation of nations. It is a nation of people with different history, culture, language and background. The country is not just like every other nation, it one with a difference. Knowledge of Nigeria will help Nigerians understand why her socio-political permutations need some sense of caution.

Several factors are considered in the development of a nation like Nigeria. Even though, America and Nigeria are nations alike, there are differences in their levels of development. The maturity levels of these United Nations determine their stability. Some of these factors that should be considered include the mindset of the people, the value system of the nation, and the country's level of development. Given Nigeria's level of development, it should operate like a family where everyone is

∧∧∧

carried along. High sensitivity on the part of the leadership is required because of its fragility. Equal treatment is needed for every member of the family to live together in unity and work for a common goal. This is necessary because there must be a sense of oneness for the people to invest in common goal.

The sensitive nature of the country requires everybody to be given a sense of belonging. It's obvious that the difference the nation can make is dependent on how we manage our strengths and weaknesses. We can be strong or weak by the strength of our state of mind. A determined mind build but corrupt mind destroys. In this regards, the mind functions as a two edged sword.

It is possible to convert the so - called limitations to strength. This is because the same weapon that is used to destroy can be use to build. The difference between the gun in the hands of a police man and the one in the hands of a robber is the orientation of their minds. The Police use guns to preserve and protect life and armed robbers use guns to destroy life. What is used to destroy can preserve if we change our mindsets. Our state of mind is what matters most.

Change is possible when we change our attitude. Obviously, we can use our differences to make Nigeria a better nation if our mindset is right. The diversity of Nigeria can be to our advantage when the motive is right. We are delicate because we have the potential to manage fragility. Why you cannot give a child bigger task is because you know he lacks the ability to manage it. Demanding assignment are for tough people and smaller tasks are for lesser beings. The food of the elephant is not given to an ant. We receive things in the measure of our abilities. Therefore, our differences rest in our strength. What is seen as limitation is strength in disguise.

Nigerians have all it takes to make Nigeria a better nation. What we need is to change our mindset so that we can make proper use of the blessings. Fellow Nigerians, the new dawn is here! As we make a centenary, let's rise with strong resilience and make a better Nigeria for our good. The old unproductive mindset has gone and the new has begun. Gladly join us on the journey.

CHAPTER ONE
NIGERIA

Nigeria, Africa's most populous country and eight most populous countries in the world is one indivisible and indissoluble sovereign state officially named the Federal Republic of Nigeria. This Federated Constitutional Republic of most populous country of the black race located in sub-Saharan Africa consists of States and a Federal Capital Territory. The independent state of Nigeria is geographically located at the extreme corner of the Gulf of Guinea, and is the largest geographical unit in West Africa. The country is situated at latitude 4oN – 14oN and longitude 3oE – 15oE of the equator within the tropical zone.

Nigeria constantly enjoys warm weather except during the rainy and harmattan seasons. Nigeria is bounded on the West by the Benin Republic, to the North-West by the Niger Republic, to the North-East by Chad Republic, to the East by the Republic of Cameroon and to the South by the Atlantic Ocean. The land area is about 923,768km2, 2013 United Nation population estimation of 174,507,539 people; monetary unit is Naira and an international dialing code of +234.

27th May, 1967 the four regions were further sub-divided into 12 States by General Yakubu Gowon. General Murtala Mohammed expanded it on 3rd February, 1976 to 19 States. 23rd September, 1987 General Ibrahim Badamasi Babangida increased the States to 21 and on 27th August, 1991 nine more States were added by Ibrahim Babangida to make states of the federation 30. 1st October, 1996 General Sani Abacha created 6 additional States to make the total States in the federation 36 with a Federal Capital Territory.

Federal Republic of Nigeria is made up of six geopolitical zones; the South - South, South - East, South - West, North - East, North - West and North - Central. These zones comprise 8, 540 Local Wards, 774 Local Government Areas, 1, 205 State Constituencies, 360 Federal Constituencies, 109 Senatorial Districts, 36 States and a Federal Capital Territory, Abuja. The power of this Democratic Republic is vested in the Executive, Legislative and Judicial Arms of Government.

∧∧∧

From the foregoing therefore, the history of the Capital City of Nigeria begins from Badagry to Calabar, Calabar to Lokoja, Lokoja to Lagos and Lagos to Abuja. Lagos as the Capital of Nigeria was adopted by the British Colonial government in the year 1914 as our Capital City marking the amalgamation of Nigeria. Lagos otherwise known as the Center of Excellence has since existed as the Capital of Nigeria until 12th December, 1991when the then President, General Ibrahim Babangida moved the Capital from Lagos to Abuja.

Portuguese explorers were the first Europeans to set feet in the Country before the emergence of the name, Nigeria. A Portuguese named Ruys De Sequilla renamed the City of Eko (Lagos) in 1472 after the Portuguese town of Lagos, in Algarre. By 1820 Britain began the occupation of the land and moved their Center of Administration from Badagry to Calabar in 1843. The Centre of Administration was again moved from Calabar to Lokoja in 1906.

Britain conquered Lagos in 1851 and in 1861 Lagos was ceded to the British by King Docemo. Lagos became part of the Gold Coast British Colony in 1874. In January, 1901 the nation became a British Protectorate. In 1912 Lord Fredrick Lugard appointed Governors for both Northern and Southern Nigeria.

By 1914 the Northern and Southern Protectorates, including the Lagos Colony were amalgamated to form a British Colony, an exercise which resulted in the emergence of the nation known today as Nigeria. January, 1914 was the month when the nation Nigeria was born and Mrs. Flora Lugard named her after the nation's major river - Niger. Nigeria literally means Niger area. In 1898 the name Nigeria was coined by Flora Shaw who later got married to Lord Lugard. Nigeria was ruled through the strategy of Direct Rule for the Southern Protectorate and Indirect Rule for the Northern Protectorate. The sixty years of the British Colonial Rule in Nigeria are characterized by frequent reclassifying of different regions for administrative purposes.

In the late 1950s African political structure was gradually achieved. 1st October, 1954 Nigeria became a federation under a Governor – General and by 1957 a federal prime minister was appointed. The Western, Eastern and Northern regions were granted internal self - government. This led to her division into Northern, Eastern and Western and Mid Western regions; each with its own House of Assembly. The premiers of these regions from 1st October 1954 – 16th January, 1966 were; Sir Ahmadu Bello - the premier of the Northern Region, Chief Samuel L. Akintola (Mid Western), Chief Obafemi Awolowo (Western) and Dr Michael Okpara (Eastern Region). 15 December 1960 – 16th January, 1966 governors of these regions were; Sir Francis Akanu Ibiam (Eastern Region), Sir Adesoji Aderemi (Western Region), Chief Samuel J. Mariere (Mid Western Region) and Sir Kazeem Ibrahim (Northern Region).

On the 1st of October, 1960 Federation of Nigeria became sovereign and independent and a member of the Commonwealth of Nations under a parliamentary government. This tenuous independent federation had an indigenous Governor – General and a Prime Minster. Dr. Nnamdi Azikiwe served as the Governor – General of the federation and known as the one who performed the ceremonial functions while Alhaji Abubakar Tafawa Balewa - the elected head of government performed the actual executive functions as leader of the coalition government of a parliamentary system.

On the 1st of October, 1963 Nigeria broke away from the British Monarchy and became a Republic. The American Presidential System of Government led to the election of Dr. Nnamdi Azikiwe as the 1st President of the Federal Republic of Nigeria. The unsuccessful coup led by Major Chukwuma Kaduna Nzeogwu resulted in the fall of the first republic on January 15, 1966 and on the 16th of January, 1966 the military took over the government. General Johnson Aguiyi-Ironsi was the first military Head of State and Supreme Commander of the Federal Republic. 29th July, 1966 there was a counter coup that led to the fall of the first Military Government as another military government was formed and Lt. Col Yakubu Gowon became the second military Head of State on 1st August, 1966.

The resultant incessant military coups led to Nigeria's civil war on May 30, 1967. Lt. Col Chukwuemeka Odumegwu Ojukwu, Military Governor of Eastern Nigeria, declared his Province an Independent Republic called Biafra. Two main characters in the bloody civil war that led to the death of about three million people are General Yakubu Gowon – the Head of State of the Federal Republic of Nigeria and his counterpart Chukwuemeka Odumegwu Ojukwu – the Leader of the Biafra Republic. January 12, 1970 Biafran leaders surrendered, as the officer administrating the government, General Philip Effiong called for a cease – fire. The seceded region was reintegrated into Nigeria. On 29th July, 1975 General Yakubu Gowon's government was overthrown by General Murtala Muhammed in a bloodless coup. On 13th February, 1976 General Murtala Muhammed was killed in a

∧∧∧

failed military coup and his deputy, Lt General Olusegun Obasanjo took over and handed over power on October 1, 1979 to Alhaji Shehu Shagari.

December 31, 1983 the Second Republic was toppled through a military coup and Major General Muhammadu Buhari emerged the Chairman of the Supreme Military Council (SMC) and Head of State of Nigeria. August 27, 1985 Major General Ibrahim Babangida ousted General Muhammadu Buhari in a bloodless coup. Babangida became the President and Chairman of the Armed Forces Ruling Council. June 12, 1993 General Ibrahim Babangida reneged on handover plan and annulled presidential poll adjudged to have been won by businessman, Moshood Abiola. August 26, 1993 General Ibrahim Babangida stepped down following massive protests against his administration, and Chief Ernest Shonekan assumed the office as head of interim government. 17th November, 1993 General Sani Abacha seized power from Chief Ernest Shonekan and became the Head of State and Chairman Provisional Ruling Council but died suddenly, making way for Major General Abdulsalami Abubakar to assume office on 8th June, 1998.

Nigeria subsequently return to civil rule on 29th May, 1999 as General Abdulsalami

Abubakar ceded power to the 3rd elected Civilian President - Chief Olusegun Obasanjo. The presidential system of government seems to as the best system of governance since the country's return to civilian rule on 29th May, 1999 if considered its basic tenets, and checks and balances of the system. Since then to date, the country has experienced uninterrupted democratic dispensation. There has been relative stability in the various transitions of government.

29th May, 2007 Alhaji Umaru Yar'adua was sworn in as President of the Federal Republic of Nigeria. Yar' Adua was the 13th Head of State of Nigeria and 4th elected President of the Republic. Alhaji Umaru Yar'adua died on 5th May, 2010 and the then Vice President, Dr. Goodluck Ebele Azikiwe Jonathan who was already acting in his stead was sworn in as President of the Federal Republic of Nigeria on 6th May, 2010. Dr Goodluck Jonathan is the 14th Head of State of Federal Republic of Nigeria.

The history of the people that constitute the present states of Nigeria dates back more than 2000 years. The earliest archaeological findings reveals that the Noks inhabited the central Jos Plateau between 300 B.C and 200 A. D. Archaeological research, pioneered by Thurstan Shaw and Daniels, has shown that people were already living in southwestern Nigeria (specifically Iwo – Eleru) as early as 900 B. C and perhaps earlier at Ugwuelle – Uturu in southeastern Nigeria, where microliths were used. Smelting furnaces at Taruga dating from the 4th century B.C provide the oldest evidence of metal working in archaeology. A number of states or kingdoms with contemporary ethnic groups were identified to have existed before 1500 years. Of these kingdoms, the three dominant regional groups were the Hausa people in the savanna, the Yoruba people in the West and the Igbo people in the rain forest region.

Nigeria is composed of more than 250 ethnic groups with over 500 indigenous languages scattered all over the country on the six geo-political zones. Igbo, Hausa and Yoruba are the three major indigenous languages while English language is used as the lingua franca. The Hausa- Fulani speaking people, Yoruba speaking people and the Igbo speaking people are represented by the acronym of WAZOBIA- meaning WA for Yoruba word for come, ZO for the Hausa-Fulani for come and BIA for the Igbo people of the Eastern Nigeria for come. The Nigeria Coat of Arms, National Flag, National Anthem, National Pledge, Nigerian Currency, Nigerian Constitution, NYSC, Unity Schools, Highways, etc are the symbols of National Unity created towards achieving unity in diversity.

Nigeria's National Flag has two colors, Green and White; the green represents agriculture while the white represents unity and peace. The Coat of Arms of Nigeria has a black shield with two white stripes that come together like the letter "Y". These represent the two main rivers flowing through Nigeria: the Benue and the Niger Rivers. The black shield represents Nigeria's good earth while the two white horses on each side represent dignity. The eagle represents strength. The yellow flowers at the base (incorrectly shown as red in the image) are Costus Spectabilis, Nigeria's national flower. Motto: Unity and Faith, Peace and Progress.

The land of Nigeria is blessed with abundant rich resources and good natural conditions. The country is beautified with people of different ethno-cultural and religious dimensions. What a blessed nation that is decorated with so many colors! This is strength in diversity! People of different religion, culture and history coming to live together as one for a common goal! No wonder she is seen as a place of unlimited opportunities by those who know the vastness of her potentials, in this regard, Nigeria is not just a nation but can be fondly described as THE NATION OF NATIONS.

^^^

Nigeria – a nation made up of nations remain indivisible as one strong nation. This uniqueness is enough to give her a place in the comity of nations. What a glorious nation we've found ourselves in! Therefore, come let's make Nigeria what she is supposed to be, a truly great nation. The strength of the country is in her unity in diversity. The more united the stronger the nation. Outstanding results are achieved when people of different inclinations work together as one. The ability to harness the vast potentials of our people is the secret of any great nation.

A cursory look at the country will show that the true Nigeria has not been revealed. If judged from the matrix of her development, what we see now is not the true Nigeria. Many a time people sing the National Anthem and recite the Pledge yet they betray the clarion call of commitment to the service of their fatherland. The objectives of unity in diversity are defeated when the people are not patriotic. What brings about development is the love one has for his/her country. There is need we think of what to do for our country rather than what the country will do for us.

How can people work for a common goal when they are not patriotic? There is need to create an enabling environment for growth even as the wind of change is blowing. We should be mindful that nation building is a collective venture. Even though the country we had wanted has not emerged, Nigeria is developing to the emergence of the true Nigeria. Given that corruption is the bare of our society and people that change from morality to immorality lives in corruption and underdevelopment. There is need for us to do things right. This is necessary to ameliorate the deplorable conditions of things because wrong doings can become legitimate if the system condones it. A mal-functional system can make a person who does wrong to think that he is doing the right thing. This could be one of the reasons some find it difficult to do things right.

Munroe, 2006 identified that whatever becomes accepted as a norm in our society eventually becomes a law of our society. If we are exposed to a certain unaccustomed or behavior long enough, we eventually become so used to it that we start to accept it. Once we accept it, we begin to think of it as "normal" or as a "norm". And once we see it as a norm, we start to expect it. Once we come to expect it, it becomes in practical terms no different from a law, even if it is never formally established as a legal statute.

In most cases, a moral code consists of both written and unwritten standards. The written standards are expressed through laws and statutes while the unwritten standards are transmitted primarily through traditions, customs, and culture. The most powerful law of all is the unwritten laws. In any culture, customs generally carry the social force of law even without formal legal establishment. And customs quite often have a greater influence on people's behavior than any formal laws that are on the books.

What is our culture? If culture deals with the language, ideas and values of a people or a nation, what is our value as Nigerians? It is also important to restate that custom is deriving from a nation's shared values. Therefore, to make a developed - free corruption nation will demand that right information forms our value system. There is the information we need to have the right mindset and develop as a nation. It is not all information that makes for development. Negative pieces of information received can accentuate corruption and underdevelopment in society. An improved Nigerian would bring about better Nigeria. Therefore, all hands must be on deck even as Nigerians from the north, south, east and west harness their strength in an uncommon synergy to build a more united Nation.

We have the resources, the people, and all that will make us a developed nation, why are people corrupt and the nation underdeveloped?

CHAPTER TWO
VALUE SYSTEM AND MINDSET

A value could be a piece of information or anything or object which the mind holds dear, just as the word which captures the mind can be regarded as a value. Our core values are things that control our thoughts, speech and behavior. In support of this, Munroe says "our values define our attitudes, behavior, and view of the world". The very information that forms our system is regarded as our value. We can create a new system by receiving new word. Word creates world; therefore, the world we want is determined by the word we receive. If it is so, then a developing nation that wants to be free from corruption and underdevelopment will need information that will make her free from corruption and underdevelopment. A new Nigeria comes by new information. The making of a new Nigeria is synonymous to giving a new word. A word or information is a value while the world created by the word is a system. Somebody's character is a product of his value and the system is the

^^^

predominant information of a given environment.

The word 'system' can be likened to the background for operation. System is the operational principle that prevails in a given society. This is like the channel created for water to flow. Just as the river channel controls the flow of water so does a system controls human behavior. A physical barrier can be created to change people course. This type of change that results from walls and roads can be seen as the architectural influence on human behaviors. Somebody can create a route to make people take the path and one who follows the path will definitely end at the destination of the road.

Man's behavior is programmed by a system. Human's behavior can be learned and unlearned. Therefore, somebody's behavior can be programmed to work in a particular direction. That is why you can know where somebody comes through his behaviors. System is the reason people unconsciously do what they do. Human's behavior and mindset are controlled by a system. That is what connects the value with the mind whereas mindset deals with the information received.

System can also be described as the programming of human mind to perform a particular function. Somebody has a mindset when his mind is set on something and the mind works in the direction of the value system. It takes the word received to forge a mindset. A neutral mind is the mind without a word and where there is no word there is no world because it takes a word to create a system.

The relationship between value, system and mindset is that information creates influence that affects the mind. A value is not just information but controlling information in the mind. The type of information spreading in a region is the value system of that place. A change of mindset will require a change of value system. The mind cannot value something without first receiving information from the system because it is the information received that is reproduced in the mind. Therefore, a system that makes finished goods its value will reproduce finished goods' minded people and the system that makes creativity its value will reproduce creative minded people. The minds of people are controlled by the system and the type of system is formed by the value the people received.

If a people present finished goods as value the environment will become controlled by finished goods system. For instance, the system that projects cars, houses, certificates and money as its value is a finished goods system because these aforementioned items are products. Somebody that comes into finished goods environment will discover that the people are measured by their number of cars, houses, certificates etc. A stranger in this environment will not need anybody to tell him the value because the positive information on finished goods will be obvious as it is seen in the people. The evidence of the value system of operation cannot be hid from their behavior. What we give but do not receive does not attract the mind of the people and if it cannot attract minds it is not the value present.

The information that attracts the minds of a people is the value system of the people. This information is the information we receive and give. Information received is the value of a place. What type of information are we presenting? There is something that makes people behave the way they do. The value system of a country makes the people to do what they do. Finished goods become our value when the information in the mind is finished goods.

The information that controls the mind is the true information. There is lot of information spreading in the society. Somebody can say that Nigeria is full of religious bodies yet the rate of corruption is high. This is so because the moral information given by these bodies has not captured the mind. It is the word one believes that he does. Students cheat in the exam because they believe it will make them

17 |*(Solutions to Corruption and Underdevelopment)*

pass the exam. People don't do the word they do not believe. Somebody is corrupt because he believes in corruption. People are corrupt when they receive corrupt information. Some of the things that can make one receive corrupt information are those corrupt acts that work in the society. People are corrupt when they see the exploits of the corrupt words the heard. We can know this from what is prevalent in that place. When you don't do what you say people will have no reason to do your word because they see it as false.

It is the information receive that forms the mindset of the people. Somebody is corrupt because of the corrupt information in his mind. There is nobody who is born corrupt. Behaviorists say that man is not innately good or bad because he is born with blank mind. The mind of a new born child is (tabula rasa) empty without a word. It is the information imparted to him that forms his personality. People behave differently because of their orientation. The vices in the country are results of negative information in the mind. We are born to succeed our predecessors just as children watch the behaviors of their elders and follow suit. The path taken by the child is the pattern chartered by the system. People are products of the system. Man is a product of the information received. Word creates system and the system creates mindset. We are

∧∧∧

products of our value system. Therefore, the information that has not captured the mind cannot make a change.

The behavior of a magnet and iron filing is likened to that of the value system and mindset. The effect of a bar magnet on an iron filing is the effect of a value on our mind. We can correlate the value with a bar magnet, value system with magnetic field and the mindset with the direction of iron filing. As the magnet attracts iron filing in its field so does the value attracts the minds in its system. Our values in life determine our behaviors. The words we receive make us behave the way we do. How somebody interprets things is also the product of the word he or she receives. People are depressed when they fail because the word received tells them that failure is not good. The way we think determines how we respond to events. That is why behavior can be learned and unlearned by words.

For instance, magnetic field is the area where magnetic force is felt. Put differently, the areas under a magnetic influence are a magnetic field. This magnetic field is analogous to the value system of a nation. The value system of a nation is the regions where the value has influence; in other words, it is the region where the force of the value is felt. If the force of finished goods is felt in Nigeria then it means that Nigeria is

19 |*(Solutions to Corruption and Underdevelopment)*

the field of finished goods. This is so because the mind of the people in this geographical area will be attracted by the value. Just as the magnet attracts every iron filing within it field so do the values (finished goods) attract every mind in it system. The state of any nation is her value.

The two types of values that affect a nation are creativity and finished goods. The preference of either of these forms can make and mar a people. People that treasure creativity are developed by the mind and those that treasure finished goods are corrupt and underdeveloped by the mind too. Man's heart is on his treasure. Creativity and finished goods are two types of values that form different mindsets. The mindset of creativity gives and the mindset of finished goods received. A nation is not truly independent when the mindset of the people is predominantly finished goods. There is the world of creativity and the world of finished goods. These worlds are different and opposite. Creative minded nations are producers while the finished goods' minded nations are consumers. When we compare creativity and finished goods we will discover that it takes creativity to develop a nation. Creative minds think on how to make things better but the finished goods minds think of how to consume.

The results of creativity and finished goods are that the creative mind creates finished

∧∧∧

goods and the finished goods minds lead to corruption and underdevelopment. Progression of the sequence is from finished goods to creativity and the retrogression of the sequence is from creativity to finished goods. The bane of finished goods minded people is underdevelopment. Therefore, Developed Countries achieve growth by moving from finished goods to creative system. Building creative mindset in the citizenry is the ladder for development of any nation. Creative minds are owners of finished goods and the finished goods' minds are expert in corruption and underdevelopment. It takes creativity to truly own finished goods.

Somebody who is creative has finished goods and the person who is of the finished goods mind lacks creativity. There are no developed inventions in finished goods' system. How can one make good inventions when the ability is latent? The factor that engineers the good things of life is creativity. This means one who goes after finished goods chases shadows because the real thing is creativity. It embodies the life of fulfillment. Creative nations determine the economy of nations that are finished goods minded because they have the value for development.

Creativity deals with making something out of nothing or something. What motivates people to do productive work is creativity. It is the necessity for finished goods that brings inventions. Cars, houses, money and the rest of finished goods are products of creativity. Finished goods are important because they are invented for comfort and rest. They are invented to ease life of stress and tension. The achievements of creativity are comfort and rest. A creative mind is a satisfied mind. That is why creative minds are not corrupt because corruption is a product of unsatisfied mind.

It is creativity that makes people to love. The heart to die for the good of people is the creative mind. That is where the inventions that bring comfort and rest come. Creative mind is what can make nations without rich resources develop. Creativity deals with innovations and one's ability to make things better. The world of invention is a creative world.

Finished goods are man-made. The expression 'finished goods' means 'finished work' and the work that is finished does not motivate people to do more work. Finished goods call for false rest. The rest is false because the people are resting when they should be working. Man is made to rest after work. Humans are not programmed to rest without work. That is why one who is resting without work cannot have satisfaction. There is no true rest when the ability is suppressed.

∧∧∧

The danger of finished goods is that it makes people rest without innovative work. This type of rest enjoyed when the mental calories have not burnt is actually false. That is why the unused energy creates dissatisfaction that generates greed. The energy that is not used for development will be used for underdevelopment. Corruption results when people lust after finished goods. What under develops a country is corruption and it is dissatisfaction that makes people corrupt.

People who are finished goods minded are those whose drive is the already made products. The life of finished goods minded person is an example of what it means to reap where one did not sow. People with this mindset cannot be independent even with all the resources required for independency. This is one of the reasons some of the training and empowerment programs to make people self employed has not yield desired result. The person with a dependent mind will still be dependent after all empowerment for independent. That is why we need to deal with the mindset first.

Finished goods information creates thoughts on finished goods. These thoughts when received bound to form a mindset. Our mindsets define who we are. To this end, creativity will always produce creative minds and finished goods, finished goods minds. Cars, houses, money, certificates and the rest of man-made items are finished goods and people that made them are like gods to all who desperately need finished goods but cannot make it.

This is therefore a clarion call for Third World Countries to pay more attention to creativity of the development centers and skills in their societies. That will aid in liberating them from being perennially dependent on the advanced nations of the world for their sustenance or survival.

With the understanding of value system and mindset, study the nation and mention it values. If finished goods are your findings, then the characters of finished goods explain the reasons for corruption and underdevelopment despite the resources, people and all in store.

CHAPTER THREE
HOW TO MAKE A NEW NIGERIA

The making of a new Nigeria can be likened to soup preparation. It is one thing to have the ingredients and it is another thing to make the soup because there are people with required ingredients who cannot prepare tasty soup. It is this inability that makes such persons to buy already made food. Other Nations can only buy raw materials from us because we cannot make needed finished goods. That is why we export raw materials but turn to import even inferior finished goods. It is unfortunate that there are people even in Bauchi State of Nigeria who trek miles to sell their tubers of yam for fried yam. The picture of this people is the pitiable image of the underdeveloped nations of the world.

The president of Federal Republic of Nigeria - Dr Goodluck Ebele Jonathan once compared the live of such people with the state of the nation and said that there is no difference between a farmer who carries his tubers of yam and walk for several miles to sell them and buy fried yam in exchange for his tubers with a nation that sells its natural resources and ironically buys from others the finished goods from the same resources. People who behave this way exercise the fate of finished goods' nations in all respect. What have we achieved when we sell our raw materials to buy finished goods made from the same material? A nation is economically dependent if it cannot control her economy. It is unfortunate that our quest for finished goods has made us sacrifice our endowment and riches to make the producing nations rich. We thought we are force to reckon with yet what we do is become slaves to the creative nations. The desire for finished goods only keeps us at the mercy of creative nations. We compromised in order to measure up to the advanced society of the day, only to discover that we have lost money and resources to these producing countries. Countries with less resources are richer than us because of the amount of money expend on inferior products. The more we import finished goods the more the nation loses money.

Clearly, one who buys a car makes the manufacturer of cars rich. It is the creative idea that besets wealth creation. This, in other words, could mean that one who lacks wisdom lacks riches. Wealth is not just a product of nature. Wealth is a product of creation. We make wealth by our abilities to make things better. Somebody must be creative enough to make real wealth. That is why producing nations will always appreciate consuming nations because they are the ones that actually made them richer. Some of the reasons for the appreciation are;

- The consumers make the producer rich
- They motivate the producers to produce
- They allow producers to lord over them
- Consumers spread their products and increase market for producers
- Consumers work for producers
- Consumers enable producers to use their God giving potential
- Consumers make the life of the producers better

Appreciation is necessary because it motivates the consumers to consume more, thereby increasing the Gross Domestic Product (GDP) and Gross National Product (GNP) of the producer country. Producers support consumer projects because at the end whatever they made will be emptied in their treasury. The cycle is such that the consumers consume what the producers produced. What a level of economic dependence!

What have we achieved as the highest producers of crude oil and the highest importer of petroleum products? When we sell our raw materials to buy the finished goods made from the crude what have we made as profit? Do we gain or lose? Let's consider the following examples;

Example 1:
If we have crude oil that is worth $20/barrel in the international market and we need kerosene, fuel and gas from them to run daily activities. Instead of acquiring the needed technology to harness these non renewable rich resources that are gifts to the land, we sell the crude oil to buy its product that worth $50. How much have we made from the transaction?

Solution
Value of our crude oil per barrel = $20
The value of products that comes from this barrel of
Crude = $50
The amount made from the transaction = value of the resources − the value of the product of the resources
The amount made on this transaction = $20 − $50
= - $30

∧∧∧

In the above transaction we have lost $30 to the refiners. If a barrel of crude oil produces finished goods worth $50, then buying these goods will demand more sell of barrels. This is the way nations with rich resources are impoverished. They export riches and import poverty. That is why nations with this mentality are not rich despite their rich resources. A rich resources nation borrows $30 to buy products of their resources that worth $50.

A nation retrogresses when she sells what can make her develop to buy things that under develops her. The system is retrogressive when we live on unprocessed materials because the whole import/export relationship between raw material and finished goods is one of unequal exchange. We make more money when we sell our refined products. The ability to creatively process our raw materials and ideas is the wisdom for wealth. It is not wise to sell primary resources for finished goods because the value of raw material is low. It is the processed raw material that has a high value.

Walter (1972) identified that after Britain had begun to move ahead of the rest of Europe in the 18th century, the famous British economist Adam Smith thought it necessary to look into the causes behind the 'Wealth of Nations'. In comparison with the first, the second group can be said to be backward or underdeveloped. At all times, therefore, one of the ideas behind underdevelopment is a comparative one. A second and even more indispensable component of modern underdevelopment is that it expresses a particular relationship of exploitation: namely, the exploitation of one country by another. All of the countries named as underdeveloped in the world are exploited by others; and the underdevelopment with which the world is now pre – occupied is a product of capitalist, imperialist and colonialist exploitation. Africa and Asian societies were developing independently until they were taken over directly or indirectly by the capitalist powers.

The underdevelopment of Africa is as a result of a systemic change. The change from creativity to finished goods is the most factor that underdeveloped Africa as a whole. African countries, especially Nigeria was known to be producers of goods. For instance, the Igbos were manufacturing brass and bronze items since 9th century AD, if not earlier. This is not to talk of Egypt which is the mother of civilization. These technologies were not developed because of systemic change. The African who now lives on raw materials cannot harness his technology. People abandoned their technology when their means of living

∧∧∧

is changed to raw goods. Africa technology was stagnated when the continent began to export raw goods and importing finished goods.

According to Walter (1972), it is particularly striking that in early centuries' trades Europeans relied heavily on Indian cloths for resale in Africa, and they also purchased cloths on several parts of the West African coast for resale elsewhere. Morocco, Mauretania, Senegambia, Ivory Coast, Benin, Yorubaland and Loango were all exporters to other parts of Africa – through European middlemen. Yet, by the time that Africa entered the colonial era, it was concentrating almost entirely in the export of raw cotton and the import of manufactured cotton cloth. This remarkable reversal is tied to technological advance in Europe and stagnation of technology in Africa owing to the very trade with Europe. And in the absence of direct political control, foreign investment ensures that the natural resources and the labor of Africa produce economic value are lost to the continent.

The situation is that Africa has not yet come anywhere close to making the most of its natural wealth and most of the wealth now being produced is not being retained within Africa for the benefit of Africans. Zambia and Congo for instance produce vast quantity of copper, but that is for the benefit of Europe, North America, Japan, and now China and India. It is unfortunate that we cannot produce finished goods with our raw materials. The trading pattern where Africa provides raw materials makes the advanced world to live well through the labor of the developing world.

Honorable Minister of Mines and Steel Development - Arc Muhammed Musa Sada confirms that there was no significant revenue generated on gemstones mining even though Nigeria has good concentration of tourmaline, sapphire, gold, emerald, aquamarine, amethyst, garnet, beryl and topaz. Chief Hussein Abubakar, Galadiman Akinyele, Chief Executive of AHMU International Mining Company, and major player in solid minerals, reports in Ibadan that the solid mineral sector can produce a handsome $20billion annually, if the activities of smugglers are checked. His words, due to illegal mining and the illegal extraction of gemstones out of this country, Nigeria is losing more than $20billion annually.

The trading pattern where we sell raw materials for finished goods is not good for the development of the country. For instance, gemstones mined in Nigeria, mostly by artisans, are often smuggled out of the country in their raw form. The country that houses the mineral gains virtually nothing when more than 90% of her gemstones are exported illegally. Nigeria makes no gains from these gemstones because the system is such that there is no market for them within. How can there be market when there are no viable manufacturing industries that make use of them in the country? It is not enough to provide gemstone cutting centers and it is not even enough to provide gemstones' market because the centers will not stand the test of time if there are no manufacturing industries for jewelry. Nations which cannot process its raw materials to finished goods are underdeveloped because they lack processing technology. It is lack of processing technology that made them lost their wealth to the producing nations.

In a way, underdevelopment is a paradox. The system is manipulated in such a way that Africa becomes dependent on other nations even after independence. Nations of Africa are dependent - independent countries when they are politically independent but economically dependent. Many parts of the world that are naturally rich are actually poor and parts that are not so well off in wealth of soil and sub – soil are enjoying the highest standard of living. This situation is unsupportable. Something is wrong when a rich land becomes poor and the ones not so well endowed rich.

We need to re – orient our minds because the mindset of finished goods is the mindset of slaves. The desire for finished goods can only make us sacrifice our toil to enrich the producer nation. Despite huge deposit of rich resources the country is poor because it cannot retain wealth. We exchange riches for liabilities when we sell primary resources to buy finished goods. That is why we will always need these technological advanced countries to make the goods acquired to work. The budget of a country goes down the drain when the people are consumers. When the citizens of a country cannot produce what they need nations that meet their needs will drain their resources.

According to Walter (1972) whatever savings are made within the economy are mainly taken abroad or are frittered away in consumption rather than being redirected to productive purposes. Much of the national income which remains within the country goes to pay individuals who are not directly involved in producing wealth but only in rendering auxiliary services – civil servants, merchants, soldiers, entertainers etc. What aggravates the situation is that more people are employed in those jobs than are really necessary to give efficient service; and to crown it all these people do not reinvest in production. They squander the wealth created by the peasants and workers by purchasing cars, whisky and perfume.

Walter went further to stress that tax do not produce national wealth and development. Wealth has to be produced out of nature – from tilling the land or mining metals or felling of trees or turning raw materials into finished products for human consumption. These things are done by the vast majority of population who are peasant and workers. There would be no incomes to tax if the laboring population did not work. The income given to civil servants, professionals, merchants, etc. comes from the store of wealth produced by community.

Example 2:

If we have crude oil worth $20/barrel in the international market but we need kerosene, fuel and gas for daily use. We use our technology to convert this barrel of crude oil to kerosene, fuel and gas. How much have we made from the transaction?

Solution

Value of our crude oil per barrel = $20
The value of products that come from this barrel of crude = $50
The amount from this transaction = the value of the product of the resources – value of the resources used

The amount made on this transaction = $50 - $20

= $30

In this transaction the country gains at least $30 because there are many other products which are of economic value outside kerosene, fuel and gas needed and the crude oil which is a gift from the land is not just capital but profit. The other products from the crude can be used to settle the cost of production.

Therefore, the actual amount made from this transaction = $20 + $30 = $50

How do we expect the country to be rich when we import virtually everything? A country blessed with rich resources may not be rich if the people are not creative enough. We can be independent economically if we harness and utilize our developmental ideas. It takes idea to rule the world. Countries that lead economically are nations that harness its ideas and technologies. Let's go beyond the mentality of dependence and become an independent nation in true sense of the word. Our freedom is from economic and political slavery. True independent is achieved when our minds are free from all forms of slavery. The vision for independent will not be achieved when our mind is economically dependent but politically independent because the true independent nation is one with both economic and political independent. Nigeria can rise beyond this limitation if only we could see opportunities in challenges. The same excuse that many give for failure is the very thing that propels people with the right frame of mind for success. Things that stand as obstacles could be your real opportunity to succeed.

Going by history, it was because the Europeans were deprived of the short – route by land to the Far East, by the Seljuk Turks, a Muslim group that they started looking for a sea – route to India. This led to the founding of a new place by Christopher Columbus which Amerigo De Vespucci later gave the name "America". In the same manner, Russia was in a serious economic mess for about 27 years. The situation led her citizen's use their brains for productivity and today, Russia is one of the super powers. Also, the entire population of China was once starving to death. Now China, with the highest population in the world, does not only have abundant food for her people but also exports food to other countries. The same applies to Japan that is currently one of the world's technological giants. For example, after the Second World War, the world was ruled by technology. A country like Japan then had no technology but people. She put her people to work, acquired the technology and excelled so much that now she is one of the world's greatest giants in technological development. If Japan and other aforementioned countries can do it Nigeria will not be an exception.

The problem of Nigeria is not far from the solution. Corruption and underdevelopment are not unique with us because every country has her problems. As population increase so does people have more ability to create and solve problems. Somebody can be seen as problem if he could not develop his ability for solution since man has the ability to solve and create problems. The act of solving and creating problems are choice. We enter into problem of corruption and underdevelopment because we receive underdeveloped and corrupt knowledge. What we need to be free is the right knowledge.

We have the resources so what we need to solve the problem of making should include technology transfer. The best way to do what you could not do is learn. Somebody who cannot prepare soup knows how to make soup by learning from those who can. It is foolishness to keep selling our raw materials to buy finished goods. What we need is not products but the technology for making Nigeria branded products so as to make Nigeria and the world better.

Renewable resources are given as gift to manage. A proverb by a Kenyan states 'treat the earth well. It was not given to you by your parents; it was loaned to you by your children'. It is myopic to use something and expect it the same because things are not made to be static in nature. It is even more myopic to think that things will remain the same in the changing world. For instance, aside our growing population, the natural plants and animals that thrives 100years ago might find it difficult to survive this time because of the change in the climatic condition. We don't expect them to be the same when their soil, food and habitat have changed. A change in the ecosystem has great effect in their lives.

We are made to make things better or worse. As we increase in population these resources decrease because we directly and indirectly affect them. That is why we should work and develop technology that makes the renewable resources serve as substitutes for the non renewable. There is need to plan on how to develop credible alternatives because crude oil does not last forever. It is not wise to depend on non – renewable resources. We need to develop a high level production technology to be able to survive beyond crude and its likes. There are so many plants and animals that would have extinct if not preserved. When we compare domesticated animals and wild life we will discover that the latter are on the verge of extinction. That is why game reserves are made to preserve them.

We have the responsibility to produce as we consume. Man was given brain to think. Common sense should teach us to adjust to the demands of changing world. We work in order to produce. There is no significant work done if the ratio of production is equal to consumption. We need to grow our agriculture to industry. It takes a large skilled people to make an industrial economy function. A business that is not profitable will not impact positively on the economy of the nation. Efficient work is done when production far outweighs consumption. Work is done when you produce more than you consume. It is not enough to cultivate because there are activities that are not productive. We don't apply crude farming techniques to feed the increasing population. What was obtainable then might not be possible today because of change.

High technical system of production is required to meet the challenges of the changing world. Not developing high tech - mechanics can make us lose what we could have made better. We can breed a better system by changing our investment climate. A good biotechnical mechanics can make a nation whose 10% of her population famers supply food to nations whose 90% of her population are farmers. High mechanized system of farming produces more than the local undeveloped system. Therefore, there is need to employ the latest technology to embrace knowledge and productivity.

Lack of technological development can make the products of a high level Nigerian professional to fall below per with that of an unskilled Chinese subsidiary. It is unfortunate that despite our levels of education we make inventions that do not meet needs of time. If an unskilled Chinese can produce a marketable products, why can't we achieve the same feat by depending on our research abilities? Our local inventions should solve the need of time.

Business opportunities are for the emerging economy. The upcoming economy has more markets for their goods especially in Africa. Even though Africa is said to be the market for finished goods and the European world market for raw materials, the continent of Africa is a world market. Many products of the developed world with high value currency are not affordable. Countries with low value of currency easily spread their products round the world because of their affordability. The economy of the world points towards creative countries with low value currency. Therefore, Nigeria can become major economy hoop when Nigerians can produce the finished goods that meet current acceptable standard. If we can produce good items that are relevant to the contemporary age then, developing and developed countries will prefer our goods.

If Nigeria can be competitive in the use of technology like the countries of China, Japan, America, Europe, etc then its developmental statues will rise beyond comparison because she has all needed to make for development. Aside the fact that China makes products of varied quality in order to meet different needs; countries patronize Chinese products because of the value of their currency. As long as the product is durable and meets demand, great number of people will always patronize cheap products.

Most times, when the market is competitive, countries devalue their currencies to increase the demand of their products. For instance, Nigeria which depend on the crude oil as its major source of revenue have to devalue Naira against dollar to maintain the demand of Nigeria crude in the foreign market as the price of crude oil falls in the international market.

TECHNOLOGY TRANSFER

Technology transfer is the process of sharing of skills, knowledge, technologies, method of manufacturing and facilities, among governments and other institutions to ensure that scientific and technological developments are accessible to a wider range of users who can then further develop and exploit the technology into products, processes, applications, materials or services.

The need for technology transfer to less developed countries from the developed countries arises on the following grounds.
1.   To overcome backwardness.
2.   To increase productivity
3.   To reduce poverty, inequalities and unemployment
4.   To increase the growth rate
5.   To fill technological gap
6.   To develop basic and key industries, and infrastructure.
7.   To make less developed countries competitive
8.   To solve balance of payment problem
9.   To solve economic problems
10.   To save time and money.
The less developed countries need technology transfer for rapid and all round economic development. It is essential for increasing the productivity of men and machines, for building infrastructure, developing agriculture and industry so as to make them internationally competitive, for exploiting and making an optimal use of their natural resources, and for developing

labor, organizational, administrative and entrepreneurial skills etc (Jhingan, 2008).

The above shows that the primary aim of technology transfer is development. Ideas are shared to facilitate rapid development. Through technology transfer we can develop our technical skills and industries. This, in other words, means that nations that work toward development can access technology by identifying new technologies, protecting technologies through patent and copyrights, forming development and commercialization strategies such as making licensing to existing private sector companies or creating new start-up companies based on the technology.

Technology and skills can also be accessed through migration from one country to another. If the country's level of development is put into consideration, Nigeria will need developed technology to continue from this communication age. Developed technology transfer will put Nigeria at forefront of development. However the challenges of technology transfer, Nigeria is not limited because she has what developed nations seek. The country does not fall below the criteria set for accessing technology. Developed and developing countries need each other for mutual benefits.

If a developing country cannot manage the technology before them then it is wise to acquire the technology for the making. This is easy as the exchange of a fraction of their natural endowment that the developed nations seek for the developed technology they need. For instance, if the condition for foreign investment in oil sector requires the deregulation of the downstream sector, then the transfer of technology to the Nigerian's subsidiary should be our priority in this agreement. We can partly trade crude oil to access the developed technology for refining. A transfer of this technology will not just develop our technology in the petroleum sector but will make us not borrow to buy refined products of our crude oil.

It is not enough to construct refinery it is enough to have the technology for setting up and maintaining refineries. Lack of this technology will make us depend on the nations with the technology for effective running of our industries. Somebody is dependent when he has a product without the knowledge of it making. The knowledge to use a product is different from the knowledge to produce the product. There is the technology for making and the technology for use.

Our professionals are handicapped when their technology is limited to usage. The technology for usage makes us consumers. We are dependent because our knowledge is in the usage. What makes a people producer is the technology for making. How can somebody not depend on the producer while he is the consumer of his products? The technology of consumption is the perpetuation of slavery. What we need is innovative knowledge for production. The technology for production is needed to power every sector of our economy.

Experts identified that Nigeria must shift from mere export of crude minerals and raw materials to manufacturer of goods possessing Nigeria seal of originality to develop. We need production technology to develop our industries and overcome the challenges of bad maintenance. What is the use of the knowledge for consuming finished goods without a commensurate knowledge for maintenance? It is not enough to buy finished goods because there is no good maintenance without the knowledge for the making. The knowledge of production or making is necessary for the development of nations.

We develop rapidly by discovering people gifted in the areas of required technology and transfer the needed developed technology in full. People with passion have the ability to bring new technology that can beat the latest technology transferred. The network for the transfer of technology needs to spread in such a way that an average Nigerian can become a maker of finished goods. This will increase both the standard of living of the people and the country's Gross Domestic Product (GDP). The establishment of the necessary infrastructures for production will boost the economy because the ability to scatter Nigerian made products round the globe will enhance the development of the country.

Talented individuals in different fields can be discovered in the fields of their passions, hobbies, and interest. Talent is best discovered when it is in a raw state. That is why parents, guidance and stewards should be mindful of the passion of their wards even at the primary level. Raw talent is discovered by making people do what they love to do in their own ways. Schools, corporate and private organizations can do better in discovering these uncommon abilities in people.

TRANSFER OF TECHNOLOGY TO CHINA

Many European companies are keen to enter the Chinese market and develop long-term partnerships in China. In order to achieve this, they are often willing to transfer their latest technology to Chinese subsidiaries of European firms and joint ventures partners. Such technology may unwittingly result in the loss of competitiveness, and market share in the mind to long term.

The common condition for access to Chinese market is as follows: Compulsory joint ventures in exchange for market access, for access to the Chinese market in some designated sectors, such as car manufacturing or the manufacturing of railway locomotives and rolling stock, demand foreign companies to enter into joint ventures with Chinese companies. Approval to form a joint venture operation may depend on the supply of specific technology, including future improvements of this technology.

In order to take part in public tenders, foreign companies must ensure that part of their production is local (in some case this can be up to 80%), Production by foreign subsidiaries in China is often not considered as local; instead, foreign firms have to work with a Chinese general contractor to which their technology has to be transferred in full.

In addition to specific rules about bidding requirements for technology transfer, China's market size is often used as a justification in the bidding process to give the contract to whichever company promises greatest transfer of know-how.

In addition to transferring detailed technological documentation, foreign companies often have to train Chinese staff so that, in future, they can design the machinery/equipment independently (China IPR SME Help desk)

∧∧∧

In the above technology transfer, the strategies adopted by Chinese are the pathway for development. These people placed technology over what they could gain as finished goods. No wonder their rapid economic development! That is why there is an overwhelming competition of manufacturing industries in Chinese market. Access to this piece of information that makes China what it is can boost our economy. The nation of India is on the path, so we can also take the same advantage for a rapid economic development. Our association with China especially on technical matters will bring rapid economic growth.

We are in a global world, as a result of which, the development of a nation requires global minds. If nations can be positively affected by globalization, then the transfer of technology is the easiest route to achieve this feat in a short time.

CHAPTER FOUR
STEPS FOR NEW NIGERIA

The journey into new Nigeria requires change in value system and mindset. The state of a nation is a reflection of her values. Nations become the product of their values. If we change our values then we have changed our system and mindset. That is why we must redefine our own to re – orient our minds. The system and mindset of a nation depends on the value of the nation. If the cake was the value the making of the cake should be our new value. The transformation of the mind approximates a redefinition of values.

The two steps to new Nigeria are;

Step one: Talent Acknowledgment

Step two: Talent Development

STEP ONE:
TALENT ACKNOWLEDGMENT

Talent is a unique treasured gift invested on man to utilize and invest. Re-iteratively, Talent is one's inherit ability. This deals with a person's hereditary traits. There are genes that differentiate persons. Why Mr A cannot become Mr B is because of these traits. These are what we need to activate in order to leave our footpath in the sands of time. What man needs to make his environment better is this creative ability.

∧∧∧

Nature sets the pace and the environment polishes it. Talent and knowledge play significant roles in our lives. People make marks on earth by developing their potentialities. This creative ability is given to solve problems. Finished goods should not be valued than creativity because it takes the creative mind to bring finished goods to existence.

It is not enough to have resources but it is enough to have the creative ideas to make wealth. People do not just make more money with money; wisdom is required to make more money. There is wisdom for wealth. That is why a creative mind can make something with nothing and the nation without much rich endowment live on the wealth of nations so blessed with rich resources. As a nation, we need information that will make us develop our creative ability for wealth. This type of information should give us the wisdom for wealth, so that we can be wise enough to use our raw materials for wealth (i.e. harness and process them).

The wisdom for wealth is necessary because there are communities and countries with rich resources that are poor and underdeveloped because the people completely depend on them. This means of livelihood has made their power to get wealth redundant. Lack of wisdom for wealth has turned the resources for blessing a curse. When one cannot use his creative ability there is no amount of money that can make him gain wealth.

The natural endowments of the land are raw materials. If we compare raw materials and finished goods we can term the raw material 'source' and the finished goods 'products'. A raw material becomes finished goods when it is processed. This means it takes more to turn raw material to a finished goods. The value of finished goods is higher than that of raw material. That means we can increase wealth by processing raw materials. The amount of wealth made depends on the creative level of our processing. Therefore, the resources of the land are the raw materials use for wealth, finished goods are the products of wealth and idea is wealth.

Wealth is not the raw material or finished goods but the ideas, technology and people's creative abilities. A nation is poor if she cannot process her raw material because wealth is not the raw material or the finished good but the technology. Many rich resources nations are poor because they cannot process their raw materials. When human potential is not effectively utilize country will remain poor despite her natural endowment.

The life of man is powered from within. Creative ability is given for man to create, recreate and impact his world. We are not made to be limited by our environment because we possess the power to create and recreate. There is unemployment in the land because the mindset to recreate our environment is not inculcated; few inventors because the word for creativity was not given. The desire for finished goods has weakened the zeal for creativity.

How can there be invention when the mind is occupied by finished goods thoughts? It is the thought conceived in the mind that gives rise to inventions. If the mind did not think of the solution to darkness, how could Thomas Edison conceived the idea, and if the idea was not utilized, how can it become reality? The mind has to be filled with developmental thoughts to conceive developmental ideas because it is the idea nursed long enough that brings forth inventions.

One of the differences between inventors and others is that the former make use of their creative abilities while the later do not. It is what you open your mind to that you receive. An idea comes when one make himself available for such idea. It was the thought of how to solve the problem of darkness that made Thomas Edison receive the idea of an electric bulb. Somebody who opened his mind to finished goods will definitely receive corruption and underdevelopment.

People see solutions when their mindset is focused on problem solving. Those that make inventions and discoveries are people who made themselves available to solving problems. Inventors are people who open their minds to solve problems. We can do even more if we preoccupied our minds with proffering solutions to problems. There is no limitation from the inside. Our limitation is over-dependence on what we have.

The things invented or discovered came into existence through the minds of people who opened themselves to them. It is not a surprise that the people who invented those courses studied did not study them. Many great inventors were not educated yet necessity caused them to make such inventions. These inventions are not just products of knowledge even though knowledge can create ideas that give rise to them. Inventions are products of creation from the people who value creativity. The product of talent is creation and creation leads to studies that give rise to knowledge. This is the power of human innate potential.

The things studied had been in existence before the study began. It was the invention of computer that led to the study of computer engineering and computer science. We study nature to know the laws governing them. This should tell us that it takes talent to make inventions. Creativity brings things into existence. The system that acknowledges talents makes inventions for development. Let us restructure our country in such a way that it creates an enabling environment for research. We can create a nation where people positively use their brains. Research institutes should meet the need of the environment as people have the right condition to think the best ideas. This is necessary because many research works do not meet the challenges of modern time.

Higher institution of learning ought to be a place that prepares people for outside world. Graduates are trained to be the best man power for industries. That is why university should partner with industries. A centre of learning need synergy with industries because it is a body prepared to meet the needs of the outside world. It is the body that bridges the gap. University is a ground that prepares people for higher responsibilities. It is a place where leaders are raised. Somebody who attained tertiary school should be trained to handle higher tasks. That is why the yenning of industries should be met in the university. Graduates should meet the challenges of time.

There is problem when universities do not meet the demand of industries. Even more problems when our minds are on finished goods. Schools need to collaborate with relevant organizations to produce quality graduates. Lack of collaboration will make the schools not to know the needs of these organized bodies and in turn produce graduates that are not relevant to them. People are schooled to meet a need and the areas of need are the areas of relevance.

The Immigration test of year 2014 conducted by the Federal Ministry of Interior was a sure test of finished goods' mindsets. Thousands of graduates without good jobs applied for a job that needs approximately four thousand persons. To underscore the level of decadence, the test that should have been written in a hall was conducted in the stadium even the national stadium because the capacity of halls could not contain them. There were many casualties, in which case more than twenty persons were stampede to death in the process.

It is obvious that the information in the system is that people should go to school, graduate with good grades and be employed in good or well paid organizations. Unfortunately people went to school, some graduate with good grades with no good jobs. So many persons with good grades have become nuisances to the society since the job promised was not forth coming. This mindset is the reason graduates depend on the government; people carry their CVs all over the country in search of job with little

∧∧∧

or nothing to contribute for development. Workers strike in every sector is virtually as a result of this dependence mindset.

The mindset to give to the society is lacking because the information was not inculcated. The system gives the schools no choice than produce dependent minds. When the primary aim of schooling is to be dependent school will have no choice than produce dependent minds. It is unfortunate that the system has made people believed that the aim of going to school is to be employed. The system has made the mind of dependence override independent mindset.

Education raison d'etre is to liberate the mind from every form of slavery but sadly the system has turned graduates to liabilities. Many of us are too dependent for the nation to carry. We expect everything from government yet have nothing to contribute for the growth of the nation. If the weight of load outweighs the strength of the pillar, of course, the house will collapse. So many developmental projects have collapsed because of this dependency mindset. That is more reason the value system needs to be redefined to make the people pillars and not loads. It is better to make people producers than give them products because the pillar makes for development while load under develops. Nigeria needs the system that will make her proactive.

A graduate that desires to work in bank can own banks! Somebody who wants to lecture in a university can own universities. If we put the effort applied in job search to build ourselves for better, Nigeria will be a paradise. Who we are is just our state of minds and the system that acknowledges talent shall give us the mindset for development.

What a country when the information of the system is; go to school, get the best from your studies and give the best to the society! This information is a value that gives a mindset for development. One in this system will obviously think in a positive direction. A student could say; I am not going to cheat or play around but will concentrate to get the best from my studies so as to give the best and make my community, country, Africa and the world at large better. If the immigration test was in this system, the number of applicants for immigration would have been the people that have passion because the system will make people not to work for money but impact. Anyone who applies for job considers it relevance to his field of strength. This is the type of information required to change the state of the nation.

An atmosphere that showcases talent will incubate the positive ideas phantom in the mind. We need an environment that can stimulate the persistence and determination

∧∧∧

required to make inventions. People are motivated when their efforts are acknowledged. Somebody who made an invention can be motivated to do more and people who are finished goods minded can be motivated to be creative. This type of motivation is required for development.

A treasured item in a dark place cannot shine until the place is illuminated. This process will make the true value shine for recognition. Many good ideas of great minds in obscurity have died without seeing the light of the day. Light is what we need to make our country better. Schools for instance bring development because it gives a measure of light. The difference between the developed and developing nations is light. Africa is backward because of gross darkness. Information is light. That is what we need to light up the society.

So many talented people who would have been exposed internationally have died as local champions because of poor information at their disposal. The value of our product attracts mind by information. People buy what they have information on. It is information that makes people to know the importance of the value presents. Our value as a nation can shine for the world to see when they have better information about us.

Many people who would have contributed meaningfully to national development are unproductive because of lack of proper exposure. And if idea is the power to cause rapid socio – economic growth, how can the country develop when these minds are allowed to die and rot in dark places. A little support can enhance productive capacity as this redundant scarce resources shines for greater light. What it takes to light a forest is a stick of match. We must bear in mind that a lighted candle loses nothing lightening another candle. This is the essence of living. We must harness and harvest our ripe positive ideas to make a developed nation.

Nigeria does not need a shift in the economy but a stable economy. We don't need to leave the oil sector and go back to crude system of farming and mining. Agriculture will not solve the limitation of petroleum if we cannot diversify our economy. The reason the nation's economy is unstable is because it is mono-economy. In oil based economy, the country experiences instability when the price of oil dwindles. For instance, on 25th November, 2014; the Central Bank of Nigeria devalued the Naira at its monetary policy committee, where it also reviewed Nigeria's monetary policy rate from 12 percent to 13 percent. The Central Bank's decision to lower the value of Naira against the dollar is to strengthen the currency. Mr. Emefiele, the Central Bank

Governor noted that the devaluation of the Naira is as a result of the continued drop in global crude oil prices. A drop in oil price would have not affect our economy if it was diversified. Stable economies are diversified economy. Countries that experience real stability are those that have diversified their economy.

From a capitalist view point, monocultures commended themselves most because they made colonial economies entirely dependent on the metropolitan buyers of their produce. Monoculture of either agriculture or petroleum is a characteristic of regions falling under imperialist domination. What we need as a nation is transformation – a shift in the system. A robust economy is one where people have the potential to excel (to be rich and get national recognition) in whatever field they operate.

In Nairaland Forum somebody said the reason US is different is that it is not a one – product economy. While she is the headquarters of entertainment in the world, she is also the headquarters of academic excellence and research. It consistently encourages its doctors, engineers, scientist, lecturers, broadcasters, writers, etc to be the best by providing a conducive environment for them to practice their trades. It does not create the impression that a senator is better than a professor by paying the senator higher than the professor or giving the senator more recognition than the professor. Even though, it is glamorizes the actors and musicians, she does not give the actors or musicians impression that they are better than police constable or primary school teacher. Polities are not made so lucrative that every media person prays to be appointed a politician's press secretary. Many broadcasters earn more than politicians, so politicians can't talk down on them or buy them over. The street cleaner does her job with bride. She knows that one day she can write a book on strategic street cleaning and it will become a bestseller that earns her millions of dollars and fame. The potentials in her profession made it not necessary for her to become a musician, politician, and a contractor, or a politician before she becomes successful.

A federal system of government is one that divides the powers of government between the national (federal) government and state and local governments. The Constitutions of the United States established the federal system, also known as federalism. Under federalism, each level of government has sovereignty in some areas and shares powers with the other tiers in other areas. For example, both the federal and state governments have the power to tax. Only the federal government can declare war (www.answers.com).

^^^

Nigeria does not operate unitary government but a federated state. The aim for the division of government is to make democracy reach the people. If so be, the country need not to be strong at the center. The people need to reside at their different geopolitical zones to experience full benefits of democracy because in a democratic government, the rights and privileges of the people need not be denied as a result of location. This is so because democracy deals with the people. It is not the government of the centre or class but the people.

In an advanced democratic society, the people are not supposed to move to the Federal Capital Territory to enjoy full democracy dividends because it is an institution that serves the people. The system of democracy is completely different from that of feudalism, dictatorship, communism and socialism. A democratic government is a government that is accountable to the people. Democratic institution reaches the people because it is the government of the people, for the people and by the people. All men are equal in a true democratic government.

How can there be true democracy when the benefits of democracy are not evenly distributed? How can there be true democracy when the center is strong? The reason the strength of the economy is one sided is because of the concentration at center. Nigeria is a mono - economy because of the powers of the center. What we need to truly diversify the economy for optimal productivity is to weaken the centre. It is the weakness of the centre that strengthens other federated units and the strengthening of the center weakens the units. If the strength of the federated unit is the weakness of the centre then there is need to weaken the centre and balance the system.

All round development in the nation's aesthetic sphere demands the center to be limited to it work. That is what we need to revive the solid mineral sector, agriculture, manufacturing, education, transportation and every other field of human endeavors. The economy of the country is one sided because the system of the country is not decentralized. Federal government is the type of government whose centre is weak. The sovereignty in federal political order is non-centralized. What truly makes the country independent is the independent of her members. An independent country is a country whose states are economical and political independent.

The system of government where states depend on the allocation from the centre is not a true federalism. How can the country experience real development when her federated unites are dependent? The character of dependent federated units is the character of children. This does not make for development. Nigeria as a federated state needs independent system of government to harness her potential. True federalism can encourage competition that brings development. That is the environment we need to form a creative system. When opportunities are given for the use of potential people will have no choice than build the creative mind for harnessing their potentials. There are various sectors undeveloped as a result of the unilateral system of government.

How can the country develop when the load of the country is on oil? Imagine what will happen when load of a truck is on a sports car! Every state has something they can harness for development. There are areas of agriculture, solid minerals, petroleum, water, sun and so forth. These natural resources can be harnessed to the level of non-dependence if we are creative enough. The system where the state depends on the allocation from the centre is likely another form of slavery. Over dependence is the reason for the poor production.

Cross fertilization of ideas and strategic harnessing of diverse gifts can make a developing country with ethno-cultural diversities to have a better chance of becoming the topmost developed country of the world. Can we imagine how the earth would have been without creativity? People are making use of the finished goods to solve their needs because some persons made use of their creative abilities to bring them into existence. If the forebears did not create, what shall we use, what would we have studied and how could we acquire knowledge?

What man gives is unlimited but what man receives is limited. Man has an unlimited potential but until someone opens his mind to them he will not access them. Creative ideas are unlimited but the finished goods received are limited and no wonder people die for them because they are for the survival of the fittest. What we need to rule our world are ideas. Every man-made thing begins as an idea in the mind of someone before it becomes a reality. It takes talent to have an idea and it takes ideas to create information and finished goods. The ability to create comes from within.

Oxford Advanced Learner's Dictionary 7th Edition defined intelligence as the ability to learn, understand and think in a logical way about things; the ability to do this well. This definition shows that intelligence is required for effective learning. There is an innate ability that enables somebody to do something well. People who are intelligent are gifted in particular things. The thinking pattern of people who have intelligence in business is different from the thoughts of people who have intelligence in linguistics. Our ability to do things well is internal and the logical way of thinking is based on our field of perception.

Special education is not just the education for the gifted or disabled but for all. Even though human potential are limitless, man is a specialized being. There is something somebody is empowered to do. That is why we are different. Not been able to exploit man's full potentials have made some to be classified as gifted, average, sub-average, and non-gifted. Even if a student is not gifted analytically, he/she can be gifted otherwise. Not meeting one's demand does not mean the student is not gifted.

Many people that are intelligent in the class have failed in the outside world. Some of the people who were rated in the class as not intelligent have performed excellently outside class rooms. Intelligence is not just measured as being good in learning mathematics. Intelligence is a gift. The word intellect can be said to be the ability from the inside. There is no person without ability in the inside. Even a moron or the dullest in the class has great ability in the inside. Although there are different innate abilities people possess but these innate abilities can be said to be the class of intelligence.

The same dictionary defines intelligence test as a test to measure how well a person is able to understand and think in a logical way about things. Every field has its intelligence test. This is because man is an intelligent being. It is possible that the person that is rated low in a particular intelligence test could be rated high on another. There is difference between theory and practical. The true intelligent quotient of a person might not be justified by a particular test.

Assessment of an individual's potential will require an appropriate psychometric test even as inner strengths should determine the choice of profession. Many talents are wasting and unproductive because we view it in one direction. If talent is inherited then the right word is required to activate this latent potential. People learn but understand differently by the word they receive. Somebody can do what he could not when his potential receives the word that activates it. Ability is found inside inability; therefore, every inability is a potential ability.

One of the reasons for 'inability' is that the latent ability has not received words that activate it. The activeness of one's potential is the word. Where there is no word, one's potential is latent. It is the word that commands action. Somebody cannot do something without a word either from inside or outside. There is need for us to go beyond the levels of analytical intelligence and maximize our human resources. That is why

∧∧∧

guidance and counseling is necessary in our school system.

Omebe (2014) suggested that guidance and counseling should now shift significantly from school based guidance and counseling probably not be judged by the traditional paper and pencil tests, but by the extent to which it contributes to national development in terms of quality of life of the people. He also identified that guidance involves mapping out procedures for helping the individual to attain his full capacities. Denga (2009) advocates that before children can be channeled effectively to suitable programmes, there is need to identify their talents and other characteristics, assess them properly, counsel them sufficiently and then place them into the most suitable programmes.

Some years ago, Dr Howard Gardner came up with a new theory about intelligence. He proposed that people were much more complex than what could be revealed in an IQ test or any other standardized testing model. He argued that different people have different strengths (i.e. intelligence types).

Before this time, it was generally believed that intelligence was a single entity that was inherited. Today, most researchers believed the opposite, that there exists a multiple of intelligence that is quite independent of each other. It also now believed that each of these intelligence types comes with its own strengths and constraints.

Dr. Horward Gardner built a model of eight different intelligence types including linguistic and verbal intelligence, logical intelligence, spatial intelligence, body/movement intelligence, musical intelligence, interpersonal intelligence, and naturalist intelligence. Each of these intelligence types is located in specific regions of the brain. However, a person can be strong in several intelligence types (www.lifehack.org).

We all have different abilities to make the world better. Human Capital Development is all about harnessing human potential for profit. Nigerians have what it takes to make Nigeria better if the momentum of their lives is driven from within. If all developmental ideas and great inventions come from the inside then the life from the inside is what we need to make the world better.

People are made to solve problems and so ideas from different talents are needed for development. Together as a people we make a better nation. Solution to a problem lies in a particular intelligence and until this idea is harnessed the solution to the problem may not emerge. We all need to contribute to build a better country because the development of any nation is a shared responsibility. Intellectual prowess deals

∧∧∧

with the ability to harness these intelligent ideas.

As people are different so do the areas of gifting vary? Every nation, tribe and people has something unique within. That is why a people can be known for something. There are areas of best. The ability to do better thus manifests in areas of individual strengths. Therefore, the best way to achieve national growth is working in the fields of strength. Every human being is created to make impact; therefore, has the potential to succeed. There is an innate ability that makes people outstanding.

The inability to utilize this ability can make the educated not to make marks even in their field of studies. That is why knowledge without creativity is a limitation. People are not the best of who they are when their knowledge cannot harness their innate potential. It is the development of one's natural ability that meets the need of time.

The past is known but the future is unknown. People discover the unknown when education develops talent. The artificial ability discovers only the known while the natural ability discovers both the known and the unknown. Limitations of artificial ability will make one not to optimize his full potential. That is why education should harness the potential within. What makes a great nation is the ability to discover the unknown. An educated mind is expected to go beyond the limit of the knowledge acquired. Apart from the information received, education develops one's mental state and stirs up the creative ability in him to meet the demand of time.

A good system of education should be the type that is dynamic. We acquire latest knowledge to form a platform for development. This is necessary because we know the known to discover the unknown. The discovery of the unknown starts with the understanding of the known and what is known is the introduction of the unknown. Knowledge is the introduction of the unknown. We know to know more. The more knowledge acquired the more one discover there is more to know. We don't acquire knowledge to remain at the level; we acquire knowledge as a benched mark to move forward. Real studies begin with the discovery of the unknown. Therefore, somebody has not begun the journey of real knowledge if his mindset is the known.

Knowledge is the known while idea is the unknown. We acquire knowledge to have insight. Polished ideas are achieved through knowledge. Real system of education discovers, develops and perfects people innate potentials. A holistic system of learning makes a real man. There is need we acknowledge talent to give real values.

^^^

Knowledge is light but idea is power. The power we need to make a difference is idea and since we don't make difference in the dark that is why we need knowledge. The light of knowledge leads one to the path of success. Every light has its source and the source of knowledge is an idea.

An idea is the source of light because it gives information that becomes knowledge. There is no knowledge without idea. The requirement for creation of knowledge and finished goods is idea. A creative system can forge an environment that precipitates ideas. All that is needed to create knowledge and information is to rekindle ideas. This system is akin to switching on an electric light. Let's consider man's innate potential as the power source, idea as the charges or current flowing while knowledge and finished goods as the electric light that shines. Somebody with a creative mind can give birth to an idea that produced both knowledge and finished goods.

It is imperative we acknowledge our natural ability to make development. We are ipsofacto responsible for nation building. People develop the mindset of giving in their fields of strengths. It is the areas of strength that make people develop the mindset of giving. Development comes speedily when priority is given to fields of strengths because everybody is talented and has what he/she can do best.

Division of labor in the organs of government is imperative in maximizing the nation's productive capacity. The executive, legislative and the judicial arms of government were created for effective governance. The same applies to other areas of life. That is why most of the agencies and parastatals of government need to be deregulated for effective services. This is necessary because government is not a business oriented institute rather a body instituted for governance.

Government is an institution that ensures the well – being of the people. How can the body that is administrative thrive in business? There is no justification when an executive contract projects to himself. One becomes master of none when he is a jack of all. No wonder the wastage, inconsistencies and low production. That is the more reason those in government should not mingle in projects but leave business to those who know it.

Division of labor is necessary for the development of the nation. The neglect of fields of strength hampers development. When people's potentials are not applied positively there is every tendency they could be applied negatively. Many a time, people fight for their rights when their rights are denied. Creative environment where every talent is relevant creates no room for nefarious practices. There are people who would have constitute nuisance in the society that are highly productive because there place of strength are acknowledged.

What limits development in the third world counties are not just poor access to basic amenities and needs but provincialism and the insufficient skills in utilizing creative ideas. We live beyond limitation when we think beyond the imaginary box that limits us. People solve problems when they open their mind to solutions. The one way of doing things is a product of an idea. Multiple ideas provide several ways of doing things.

A country is underdeveloped when the minds are stereo-typed by tradition to think rigidly in one direction. It is unfortunate that the tradition of one way has weakened the motivation for creativity. What could we have done if there is no petroleum in the land? If countries like Japan and the other developed countries which are technologically advanced can thrive without depending on natural resources, Nigeria has what it takes to do even better because she is multi-potential country. What the nation needs is the creative system to unleash its potentials.

Development comes through initiatives as creativity is the foundation for growth.

While creativity builds a nation knowledge systems it. A nation is not developed by depending on the old ideas because what bring development are the new ideas. Based on the Human Development Indices, a nation must act independently in the world trade market to be called a developed country. The primary sector driven economy can only boost the income of the country and this is not enough to make a developed country.

Third World Countries are mostly those that depend on the primary sector's economy. These are nations that exchange raw goods for finished goods. Any nation that depends on unprocessed agriculture, crude oil, and solid minerals and other unrefined resources as her major source of revenue is far from becoming a developed country. This is because the resources of the land serve as the tool for development. These raw materials are not made for dependence rather that man should use them and make what they need.

Even experts identified that for Nigeria to realize her vision 2020, the country must shift from mere export of crude minerals and raw materials to manufacture goods possessing Nigeria seal of originality. This therefore means that modern development demands industrialization. Nigerians need to concentrate more on development of the manufacturing sector. Breakthrough in

∧∧∧

human development depends upon man's technical capacity to deal with his environment. A value system that acknowledges the prevail place of talent will build that productive capacity for development.

STEP TWO:
TALENT DEVELOPMENT

Man came on earth as a raw material. Every person born on earth requires some measure of development to be useful. That is why we must subject ourselves to required processes that will make us products of values. This is necessary because nothing raw has great value. A value is released when raw material is processed. That is why we need education to imbibe lasting values. The more the mind is developed the more valuable we become. A talent is a raw material that can be used for an excellent assignment when it is processed with the right information. Raw materials are for processing but products are for use. There is no much value for people who live on products that are not processed. Human Capital Development is a development for profit. Talent development can be seen as the development of human capital to maximize potential. Obasi (2008) submitted that Human Capital represents the knowledge, skills and abilities that make it possible for people to do their jobs, while Human Capital Development is about recruiting, supporting and investing in people, using a variety of means, which includes education, training, coaching, mentioning, internships, organizational development and human resources management for its eventual realization.

Talent is harnessed for production. We find some things difficult because we have not developed ourselves enough to handle them. The development of oneself enhances performance. Something that was difficult becomes easy through development. That is why somebody who wants to perform better develops himself. We develop our innate potential to give the value proportional to what we want.

The power of man's natural ability can be likened to that of money. Money is the medium for exchange. We use money to buy goods. The price of goods sold in the market depends on their values. High valued goods have high prices and the low valued goods have low prices. Somebody can be said to be poor when the values he present cannot buy the valuable goods in the market and rich if he can. Poverty deals with one's inability to give the value required to buy valuable goods sold in the market. In the same way a nation is poor when the people lack the capacity for development.

∧∧∧

We develop our potential to have the value that can buy the better things of life. Ban on importation may not effect needed change if talents are not developed. Apart from colonization which made Africans to have no much value for their products, people import because local production has not met their needs. That is why talent needs to be developed to make better goods. The development of talent enables talented individuals to make superior finished goods. The talent that is not developed results in the manufacture of substandard goods. When talents are not developed with latest knowledge the creative outputs may not meet the need of the people. What we need to stop importation of finished goods is the development of talent.

Talent development is necessary for making a better nation. The capacity to make a better nation requires the development of talent. Nigerians most develop themselves to what they want because local people makes local goods and the refined people make refined goods. People give what they have. It takes a developed mind to make developed goods. One of the things that make a rich nation is capacity building. We develop ourselves to be productive enough to meet the needs of time. Capacity building is needed to enrich our lives.

Innate Values + Acquired Values = Developed Mind

A developed mind is a renewed mind. The unwanted information in our mind have to be processed for the mind to be renewed. People achieve giant strides through capacity building. Self development gives us the ability to do what we could not. Our limitations can be conquered by self development. One of the reasons people finds it difficult to manage higher challenges is because they have not developed themselves enough. Talent development is what we need as a nation to move to the next level. Talent development makes people outstanding, and the medium for the development is education.

The certificate in character and learning somebody received after graduation from a university is a good indication that man is trained to renew his mind with information that can mold his character for good. People are measured by their level of knowledge. One's height of exposure is measured by his level of knowledge. A talented person that lacks knowledge will only be caged by the walls of his locality. Talent and knowledge are the synoquonia panecia for development. Nigeria needs to merge academic programmes with individual's natural ability to harness people's full potentials. There is something somebody can do best. Academic

^^^

work should exploit this potential in man. There should be integration of all that are required to develop talent because without revealing hidden abilities of students, the schools will be producing civilized minds with no capacity to move the nation forward. Man's liberation has to do with having more opportunities to display and develop talent. The development of one's natural ability is an intrinsic value of education.

Knowledge is necessary for development. It's the tool that solves life challenges. Man is stagnant without knowledge. People repeat those things they should have outgrown by ignorance. We need knowledge to move from one point to another. Knowledge is the key that unlocks the door of progress. In everything, we need knowledge to improve. There is no appreciable growth when we don't build on the existing structure. The essence of studying and reading is to know who we are, our environment and principles so as to build the right attitude about life. Through education and extensive use of the written word, Europeans were able to pass on to the rest of the world the scientific principles of the material world which they had discovered, as well as a body of varied philosophical reflections on man and society.

Lack of documentation is one of the factors that make African countries underdeveloped. Developed countries like the United States train people to continue where their predecessors stopped. Expansion will be necessary when one has built on an existing structure. We take over from somebody to expand and not to start a fresh project. There is no continuity when knowledge is not transferred. Many African with wealth of experience find it difficult to write and preserve their rich experience by documentation.

How can the younger generation learn without history? We should cultivate the habit of putting things on paper because it is the best way to preserve. It is through writing we can project out true cultural heritage and through writing we can develop. The best way to transfer knowledge is to put down our lessons in writing. If parents can put down their wealth of experiences on paper, their children will be better because they will build on their achievements.

People avoid the mistakes of the past when they know past successes and failures. Lack of documentation makes children to learn little of the vast experience of their parents. Our children will certainly be better when we keep records of events that shape our lives. There is no history without a record. Knowledge is the requirement for living.

∧∧∧

Just as man needs food to grow so does one needs knowledge to grow. The importance of knowledge cannot be overemphasized because man needs knowledge to even understand who he is. Man needs knowledge to discover his potential. Man begins life by learning and ends life with learning. The journey of life is all about learning; knowledge draws one out of the pit of ignorance. The power of knowledge cannot be underestimated because it creates the mindset that makes a person.

It is knowledge that keeps one away from those things that can destroy him. We can only be deceived and destroyed when we don't have knowledge. If we examine life carefully we will discover that the dark parts of life are areas of ignorance. A victim is always one who lacks knowledge of what is ahead. Knowledge makes one free. The more people acquire knowledge the more they become free from bondage. Freedom is bought by knowledge, which is why knowledge is hidden from slaves. Dictators enslave people by hiding information from them. How can you be enslaved when you understand yourself and the environment? It is knowledge that brings out the values in you. Something is wrong when the information received did not achieve the purpose of knowledge. Acquired knowledge should harness one's innate potential.

There are different types of knowledge that create different mindsets. There are the true knowledge and false knowledge. It is not all knowledge that makes for development. What makes a people corrupt is the wrong knowledge. How can I have knowledge and find it difficult to live right? If the primary aim of acquiring knowledge is the renewal of mind then I should do that which is right by my knowledge. True education breeds confidence.

The knowledge that does not bring out one's innate potential is a false knowledge. This type of knowledge enslaves. People are enslaved when they acquire knowledge that hides their potential. False knowledge can hide people's natural abilities. It does not develop talent. Low self esteem is a sign of false knowledge. It is the right knowledge that gives boldness. Any knowledge that limits you is a false knowledge. This is the type of knowledge we need to do away with because it does not make for development.

What then is your worth without a value? How can somebody be a shadow and live? We are made to live our lives from the inside. A true educated mind is somebody that lives his life from the inside. The wrong type of knowledge will definitely build the mind in the wrong direction. Some of the added values can hide one's natural ability. The wrong type of knowledge will not allow one's natural ability to come to light.

∧∧∧

Something is wrong when my knowledge keeps me in bondage! For the fact that you are not talented analytically does not make you inferior. There are different types of intelligence necessary for different fields of life. Knowledge should be applied.

Dr. Kofi Busia some years ago made the following submission. At the end of my first year at secondary school (Mfantsipim, Cape Coast, Ghana), I went home to wenchi for the Christmas vacation. I had not been home for four years, and on that visit, I became painfully aware of my isolation. I understood our community far less than the boys of my own age who had never been to school. Over the years, as I went through college and university, I felt increasingly that the education I received taught me more and more about Europe and less and less about my own society.

What meaningful contribution can one make when he is ignorant of his environment! An educated mind should affect his environment because man is not made to leave his undeveloped environment the way he met it. Something is wrong when the role of education is producing Africans that only service the capitalist system and subscribe to its values. If China can develop and commercialize its herbal medicine, Nigeria can develop her local medicine. The

Western orthodox medicine is simply a product of development.

The right knowledge is what we need. The right knowledge is the one that gives light, freedom and confidence. Right knowledge is one that activates one's innate potential and enables him to contribute positively in the society. What is called true knowledge is the knowledge that makes one live from the inside. True knowledge is the knowledge that reveals your value. This type of knowledge harness's human ability for better performance

CHAPTER FIVE
EDUCATION

Education is the means for training the mind for development. It is one of the ways of meeting human needs. This results in economic development of both individual and the society as well enables man to make meaningful contributions on socio-economic development of the society. According to Shokunbi (1999), education is the process through which ignorance is eliminated, skills for productivity and leadership acquired and the key to future productivity and comfort acquired (cited in Udida, L. A., 2010).

Education informs, develops and transforms. Development in life is as a result of education. Quality education is essential for the development of any nation. Man appreciates in value by knowledge and depreciates by ignorance. What one knows differentiates him from others. Education whether formal or informal, is made for the development of people and empowering them with the right knowledge enables them to live better.

Mathematically, education can be expressed in this form:

Education = Mental development + Knowledge

Although the mental state is developed by knowledge, in a logical definition of education, the metal capacity deals with the container and knowledge deals with the contents. It is the content that determines the container. One's level of education can be measured by his mental capacity and knowledge. The mental capacity (container) is high by knowledge (contents). It takes mental development to acquire knowledge. Man's mental capacity expands and contracts. The elasticity of man's mental state is synonymous with the expansion and contraction of muscles. The increase in the rate of physical exercise expands the muscles while decline contracts muscles. The rate and type of physical exercise determines the level of expansion.

People operate at different levels of development. There are courses for the low and high class. Even the duration of these courses increases as one goes higher. That is why courses that require high mental capacity are undertaken by people in the advanced schools. The higher the class the more advanced the course. For instance, a primary school student that understands primary school algebra may not comprehend university algebra because of the advanced nature of the university algebra. His inability to comprehend university algebra even

∧∧∧

though good at primary algebra is due to his low mental capacity. The brain that is not matured enough may not handle advanced courses. The level of his mental capacity is his level of knowledge. Mental capacity improves with knowledge. To improve in mental capacity will demand improvement in mental exercise.

Somebody's capacity to acquire knowledge depends on his level of training. We study to improve our mental capacity. The productive capacity of a person can be measured by the current state of his mental capacity and knowledge. This should be one of the reasons aged people forget a lot. The more one declines in mental training the more the person forgets and the more the person appreciates in mental training the more he remembers.

Mental stretch can be used to measure the level of mental development. Students receive the ability to learn through mental exercises. Therefore, mental development can be defined as the expansion of mental capacity. Knowledge is needed for this expansion. One does mental exercise when acquiring knowledge. Mental development measures the level of understanding and the scope of reasoning. The word 'smart' is a product of mental exercise. Just as the consistent athlete can be smart so is the one that studies regularly.

It takes the information in the mind to develop mentally. The level of development is the level of application. People don't work beyond their capacities. The capacity of a person is the level of the person's performance. If we relate mental elasticity to the catapult, we can correlate the stretch with mental capacity and the stone as the knowledge. Somebody is educated by the information in his mind. His level of knowledge depends on the level of his mental capacity.

High level mental capacity increases the ability to acquire knowledge and low level mental capacity decreases the ability to acquire knowledge. We do mental exercise when we think or solve logical questions such as mathematics. Exercise enhances the capacity of the brain. The ability to acquire and retain knowledge increases with the expansion of mental capacity and decreases with the contraction of mental capacity. A high level mental development that is not subject to intensive studies and exercise can become low while a low mental capacity subjected to intensive studying and exercise can be high. Aptly, brain cells are activated and developed by mental development.

Education makes the development of the mind possible and without it man will hardly grow mentally; growth will obviously slow down and development will almost become impossible even as successive generations

ᐱᐱᐱ

repeat the same mistakes. There is no national development without education. Life is stagnated without knowledge. The act of repeating the same thing at different times is not enough to bring about development.

We need to constantly rob minds with those who have gone ahead of us to improve on development because development is as contagious as the issues of life. Sir Isaac Newton said, 'if I have seen any further, it is because I am standing on the shoulders of those that have gone before me'. Globalization is an opportunity for developing nations to learn from the more advanced nations. It is possible in today's world that nations develop at faster rate. If developed nations spent hundreds of years to developed, Nigeria can develop at a shorter time.

EDUCATION IN NIGERIA

Education in Nigeria is an instrument "par excellence" for effecting national development. Towards achieving the national objectives, the anticipated goals of the philosophy of the national policy (2004 section 1:7-8) state as follows:

a) The inculcation of national consciousness and national unity;

b) The inculcation of the right type of values and attitudes for the survival of the

individual and the   Nigerian
society;

c)   The training of the mind in the understanding of the world around; and

d)   The acquisition of appropriate skills, abilities and competencies both mental and physical as equipment for the individual to live in and contribute to the development of the society.

The National Policy on Education enunciated the 6-3 -3-4 system of education which had its broad aims as:

1.   The acquisition of skills

2.   Provision of a wide range of subject options

3.   Selection or choice of course based on the service of guidance counselors.

4.   The promotion of morality and fair play nationalism, physical fitness and healthy living.

5.   The exposure to technical versatility.

The policy viable as it seems has experienced some drawbacks. Ikeagwugo (2000) in Shokunbi (1999) lamented that the implementation of the 6-3-3-4 was ineffective and hence the desired goals could not be achieved. 6-3-3-4 system of education was the modification of the traditional 6-5-4 system of education which was practiced in Nigeria. It was introduced in Nigeria in 1982 and based on the principles that individuals are placed in

∧∧∧

academic programmes depending on continuous, sequential, systematic, and comprehensive, guidance and counseling cum organized continuous assessment programmes. This was because the British system of education, which was practiced in Nigeria, could not meet the technological requirements needed in Africa as a whole.

The curriculum of African schools were neither in line with the existing African conditions nor consistent with the postulations of political independence. The system of education lacked a balanced economic development, including rapid industrialization. Thus, it became pertinent for the new African nations to draw up a programme of educational development that opted for innovation in the secondary school curriculum.

The 6-3-3-4 system is a multi- talent development type of education which advocated 6 years pre-vocational education in the primary school, 3 years of junior secondary and three years of senior secondary school education with vocational, technical, commercial, grammar, or teacher training education and four years where students are admitted into the university or any other tertiary institution.

The aims of the primary education as enshrined in the National Policy on Education (2004 section 4:14) are to:

1.   Inculcate permanent literacy and numeracy and ability to communicate effectively;

2.   Lay a sound basis for scientific and reflective thinking;

3.   Give citizenship education as a basis for effective participation in and contribution to the life of the society;

4.   Mould the character and develop sound attitude and morals in the child;

5.   Develop in the child the ability to adapt to the child's changing environment;

6.   Give the child opportunities for developing manipulative skills that will enable the child function   effectively in the society within the limits of the   child's capacity; and

7.   Provide the child with basic tools for further educational advancement, including preparation for trade and crafts of the locality.

Secondary education is the education children receive after primary education and before the tertiary stage (National Policy on Education document 2004 section 5:18). The broad goals of secondary education shall be to prepare students for useful living within the society and higher education.

Tertiary education covers the post-secondary section of the national educational system which is given in universities, polytechnics, colleges of technology, colleges of education, advanced training colleges, correspondence colleges and such institutions as may be allied to them. The teaching and research functions of the tertiary education are aimed at developing a high level relevant manpower and national consciousness through inter-institutional co-operation and dedicated services to the community.

The 6-3-3-4 system of education was fashioned to produce graduates who would be able to make use of their hands, head and the heart (the 3Hs of education). However, not being able to achieve these goals and the need to meet up the challenges of the time led to the new educational policy known as the 9-3-4 system of education (the Universal Basic Education).

The scheme structure provides that there should be a continuous basic education for nine years, from the primary to the junior secondary levels; three years for the senior secondary, and four years at the higher level. The contents would be directed according to NPC-NEEDS (2004) document:

1.   Towards faithful implementation of the free, compulsory Universal Basic Education law, among   others.

2.   Towards the review of school curricula from primary to tertiary so as to incorporate vocational and entrepreneurial skills, re-tooling and repositioning of

technical schools to be able to address the technical manpower needs of the economy.

3. Towards the establishment of more vocational centers to encourage Nigerians to embrace vocational education;

4. Towards the review of school curricula at all levels to incorporate the study of information and communication technology (ICT) (Udida, L. A., 2010).

A study of the National Policy on Education will attest to the viability of these policies yet the Nigerian schools have not attained the standard and accessibility envisaged by the policy statement. One of the observations in the development plans of Nigeria shows that the educational system, besides being a poor social service, lacks quality and proper orientation. The current situation is far from the ideal because the outcome of the 6-3-3-4 and even the 9-3-4 system could not meet the objectives of the policy. The fact on ground has not met the needs of the environment and the citizenry.

Asuquo (2009) identified that the major challenge facing the school today is how to give individuals the best possible opportunity to reach their full potential so as to become confident, socially productive citizens and to prepare young people to live and work in a world characterized by constant change, instability and uncertainty.

Apart from the political, economical, religious, racial, cultural, technological and developmental differences among nations, an efficient system of education which works in other countries, most especially the developed world has not worked in Nigeria because of a not so enabling value system. The discrepancy between the policy of education and its output is as a result of the value system of the country. Efforts made to actualize the policies have not yielded required results because of the system.

The system of education in the country has produced different output because the general system upon which the country operates is not conducive for its growth. It takes like to give rise to likes. Every system produces its kind. The products of a country are the result of the system of the country. This is enough to make the education received tend to the value system of the country therefore produce different output. That is why there is need to redefine our value system to thrive in education.

Nigeria needs a creative system to unleash the greatness of its citizenry. This is necessary because man is a multi-talented being who lives in a multi-dimensional environment. Apart from understanding his environment, he also needs to discover himself so as to optimize his full potential. The ability to realize his potential will make him add value to his environment. This is necessary because it is not all added values can make one add value to his environment. Some added values can hide one's natural ability. That is why the best system of education should be the type that also reveals the students hidden potential.

Asuquo (2009) also disclosed that the primary goal of guidance is to help the student develop personal autonomy and identify as well as wholesome adjustment commensurate with their innate potential. The education whose priority is not to maximize student's natural ability makes not much difference in society because it makes people to live without impact. It is just like the snake without head. Students no longer read as they should because of the value system. If the aim of going to school is to come out with good grades and be employed in a good organization then it means that people attend schools to become dependent.

EFFECTIVE SYSTEM OF EDUCATION

Effective system of education could be said to be the system of learning that meets the need of time. This system of learning is required to be abreast with the sociological and technological changes. There are changes going on all over the world. Even the earth revolves and spins round its axis. As time and knowledge progress, development demands that we constantly upgrade ourselves with latest knowledge so as not to be left behind by the train of changing world.

The evolving world of science and technology demands that education is constantly modified to suit the latest knowledge for generations to grow intellectually. When what we studied and read does not reflect societal realities, living accordingly will be difficult.

Most of the things studied in schools are no longer relevant to the present time. The courses taught in the schools need constant reviewing because many theories and laws have been modified. As things progress people learn with modifications. Discovery is a product of learning. Knowledge is acquired to bring about better knowledge. Man builds on the known to discover the unknown. The limitations of theory and laws are discovered when we have the knowledge. That is why we need to build on the latest knowledge to make better contributions.

Therefore:

Development of a Nation = Education of Time + Creativity

Stagnation of a Nation = Education of Time - Creativity

Stagnation of a Nation = Education not of Time + Creativity

Underdevelopment of a Nation = Education not of the Time – Creativity

The expression above reveals that education and talent work together to achieve common goals. Therefore, if an undeveloped mind can invent what is studied developed minds can do much better. An effective system of education is therefore defined as the education of time that harnesses human potentials for the development of the nation. To have comparative advantage in the level of knowledge demands constant adjustment to latest knowledge. The transfer of recent technology is needed to develop world- class skilled and capable manpower to power information technology, finance and social engineering.

Changing times and events demand that we are abreast of recent knowledge. The person with outdated knowledge might not be important in modern world. Graduates are not relevant to industries when the academic work does not meet the demands of industries. That is why organizations mount seminars for their workers to make them abreast with recent knowledge. Effective education is the system of learning that bridges the gap between institutions of learning and industries.

Change is said to be permanent and our system of learning is subject to it. That is the reason we need to equip ourselves with the latest knowledge to survive change. The

∧∧∧

positive changes made are the things that bring about development. Our modus operandi of operation needs to be revalued because a better system of education is possible when the finished goods system is changed to creativity.

Let us restructure our system to create enabling environment for a better system of education to thrive. We need a better system to achieve the objectives of education because system is like the soil for cultivation. Crops thrive best in the soil. We need a system where our nice polices will thrive. Our institutions produce dependent minds because the value system of the country is dependent. That is why a change of system is necessary to achieve our noble educational goals.

CHAPTER SIX
DEVELOPMENT OF NATIONS

The word 'nation', as defined in Oxford Advanced Learner's Dictionary 7th Edition is a large community of people, sharing a common history, culture and language, and living in a particular territory under one government. By this definition, it implies that 'nation' deals with people. A large community of people is required to make-up a nation, therefore, if the majority of the people are poor, the nation will be regarded as poor and if the majority of the people are rich, the nation will be regarded as rich. The position of a country is determined by the quality of living her people and not by the amount of resources. Poverty is said to be defined as the low level per capita income of a country. Therefore, a poor country does not mean a young country rather poor countries are the countries with low level per capita income.

Poverty is a product of underdevelopment. A nation that is formed or born needs adequate developmental apparatus to grow. Nation building is the processes of growing the formed nation. There is no how a country will develop when the people are poorly informed. It is malnutrition that leads to poor growth. There is the ratio of nutrient required for proper growth. Just as a child

∧∧∧

need balanced diet at the right proportion to grow well so does a nation need the right information to developed. A country becomes underdeveloped when there is no enough light for development.

Omebe (2014) noted that one could conveniently refer to development in multi – dimensional terms. That is, one cannot measure development by using only economic growth or by any other exclusive indicator. He also identified development as a condition of well-being of society as a whole.

A country blessed with many rich resources whose majority of her people are poor, is regarded as a poor nation. This results because a nation is directly proportional to the human resources. The human resource is the medium for development while other resources are the tools in the development. Development is not purely an economic affairs but an overall social process which depends upon the outcome of man's effort to deal with his natural environment. The word "development" when narrowed to economy, the average bourgeois economist defined development as simply a matter of the combination of given factors of production namely land, population, capital, technology, specialization and large – scale production.

A nation that invests in her people develops faster than others because it is the empowered citizens that catalyzed development. A nation remains underdeveloped when her people cannot contribute meaningfully for development. If the nation is not developing, it then means that the citizens are not investing in her. How can a country become developed when the people only exploit her resources? The business of exploiting the country's resources is likened to the relationship between the host and the parasite.

The mind of exploitation under develops a nation because people must invest to make development. It is investment that makes a nation grow. Stability and growth occur when people receive and give. Some of the social upheavals and endemic vices in the society result because people refused to give what they received. For instance, desert encroachment is experienced because people refuse to replace the trees cut down. When people eat but do not defecate or excrete, they die of complications. The river that does not discharge the water received stinks.

To know our problems are as easy as identifying those things we refused to give. The things we selfishly retain are the problems. People die of heart complications because they refused to release the stress that had accumulated in their systems. Overtime, Earthquakes and other natural

∧∧∧

disasters happen because of the so much accumulated energy within the earth crust. How can we expect to have peace when we refuse to give out what is not ours? It is natural to give and live. Therefore, until we receive and give, stability and growth might not be experienced, because one lives as he gives and dies as he retains.

Development is in discovering. It takes knowledge to achieve development. We can't develop without discovering the things that make us underdeveloped. The countries that spent two hundred years before becoming developed might have spent those years on experimentations. Ignorance can make somebody waste 24hrs on a journey that is less than 10minutes. One does not reach his destination if he does not know where he is going. Therefore, we are not expected to spend the same numbers of years spent by these nations that pioneered development but we can take advantage of the discoveries of developed world since their experimentation, hypothesis, theories and laws are facts. All, the developing nations need to do is to fast track their development by learning from the leagues of the advanced nations.

The development of a nation is the same as the development of an individual/person. The mind is developed by knowledge. Somebody who knows where what he needs is does not search for it. People waste time on something because of ignorance. Lack of right knowledge is the reason for underdevelopment. A country is developed because her citizens have developed themselves. Investment in people is the investment on nation. It is the development of an individual that makes the development of a nation possible. Development is not just physical structures but the people. If the number of citizens that develops themselves not equal to what make development the nation is not developed. It is better to build people than built structures because the building up of people is the building up of nation!

DEVELOPED AND DEVELOPING COUNTRIES

The term 'developed country' is used to describe countries that have high level of development according to some criteria while 'developing countries' is a term generally used to describe the nation with a low level of material well-being.

Professional economists speak of the National income of countries and the National income per capita. Information from United Nation Statistical Publications shows that it is the gap in per capita incomes that allows one group to be called developed and another underdeveloped.

The Human Development Index (HDX) measures the development of countries on three criteria:

1.   Longevity: This depicts the life expectancy at birth.

2.   Educational attainment; as measured by a combination of adult literacy (two-third weight) and   combined   primary, secondary and tertiary enrolment   ratio (one-third weight).

3.   Standard of living; as measured by real per capita (Jhingan, 2008)

Countries are rated according to their development indices (both human and economy). These   parameters   of development divide countries of the world into three:

1.   First World Countries

2.   Second World Countries

3.   Third World Countries

First World Countries

First World Countries in general have very advanced economies and very high Human Development Indices. The United Nations defined First World on the wealth of the nation's Gross National Product (GNP). This refers to the so-called developed, capitalist, industrial companies, roughly, a bloc of countries, aligned with the United States after World War II, with more or less common political and economic interest, such as; North America, Western Europe, Japan, and Australia.

Second World Countries
Second World Countries are referred to the communist-socialist industrial states, (formerly the Eastern bloc, the territory and sphere of influence of the Union of Soviet Socialist Republic) today: Russia, Eastern Europe (e.g. Poland) and some of the Turk States (e.g. Kazakhstan) as well as China.

Third World Countries
Third World Countries include all the other countries that do not belong to either of the aforementioned. Today the term is often used to roughly describe the developing countries of Africa, Asia, and Latin America as well as Capitalist (e.g. North Korea) countries, the very rich (e.g. Saudi Arabia) and very poor (e.g. Mali) countries. Third World Countries is colloquially used to describe the poorest countries in the world (Wikipedia).

These countries are classified by various indices: their political rights and civil liberties, the Gross National Income (GNI) and poverty of countries, the Human Development Indices of countries, and the freedom of information within a country (nationsonline).

∧∧∧

The Principles of World System of Development of Nations is such that some nations produce while others consume. As producers need consumers to sell their goods so do Consumers need producers for better living. If there are no consumers, producers may not have those who will buy their goods and development will be difficult to measure. This system demands that there should be market for producers and consumers. In order to successfully establish these two world markets and regulate development, there is need that some nations specialize in production while others should consume.

In this system, the consuming nations serve as the market for the producing nations and the producing nations - as market for the consuming nations. This is to enable the producers to produce what the consuming nations can consume. If there is no defined market for production and consumption, the system will not be classed properly because the defined system of development is required to form a Cycle of Development of Nations.

Nations are classed because of the defined system of development. For instance, if a nation is known to be producer, then that nation should be classed as developed, rich and First World Country, but if a nation specializes on consumption, then that nation is a developing, poor, and Third World Country. The Western World classification is challenged when nation's development is independent of the system of development of nations. For instance, the Communist - Socialist Industries States like China which are neither classed as producer or consumer as a result of their independent system of development may not be classed as rich or poor, developed or underdeveloped because of their in - between. Some of these non - specialized - independent developing Countries most especially countries that are of the Soviet Union are classed as the Second World Countries.

The system of development of nations is such that no nation is absolutely independent of others so that there could be a United Nation. The rich need the poor and the poor also need the rich. In the cycle of development of nations there is the rich and the poor nations just as the two coexist in the society. These two classes of nations are required to balance the system.

African nations are not developed because the continent - Africa and the rest of other countries especially those countries that gain independent after the formation of United Nation, were systematically drafted as markets for the producing nations. The cycle of development is such that as long as a nation consumes, that nation cannot become developed, rich and First World. The main basis for classification of a country into Third World is not poverty but consummation. If it is poverty a very rich country like Saudi Arabia would have not been classified as a Third World Country. Even the Holy Book states that it is more blessed to give than receive. The place for the producer is always at the top. Nigeria can become rich, developed and First World Country when the nation moves from the place of consumers to the place of producers.

The result of human development index which is the basic parameter for measurement of development of countries depend on the value or specialty of a country. Nations that are developed, rich and First World have high human development index while nations that are poor, developing and Third World have low human development index. One can predict development level of a nation by its value.

MINDSET OF DEVELOPED AND UNDERDEVELOPED NATIONS

There is the mindset of development and underdevelopment. It is the mindset of development that brings development and the mindset of underdevelopment brings underdevelopment. Somebody's personality is reflective of his mindset and the things that make him have his kind of mindset constitute his values. The personality of a person is the product of his values.

A value creates a system that either develops or under develops a nation. It is the mindset of development that brings development and the mindset of underdevelopment brings underdevelopment. The state of a nation is dependent on the value system of the people. If the value is creativity the system and mindset will be creative but if the value is finished goods the system and the mindset will be goods. Also, where creativity is the value, the people of that land can sacrifice their lives to make inventions that would stand the test of time and where finished goods is the value people can sacrifice their lives to acquire the best finished goods.

These differences in mindset as a result of the value system make the people of the developed world work innovatively and the people of the underdeveloped world work with the mindset to receive. The differences in values make these minds behave differently. Just as stated "man is not innately good or bad. He is born with a blank mind". people are not different because of their race they are different because of their values. It is the value that can make a person from the developing world corrupt. Obsession with finished goods is the product of the value.

We look but see differently. Where a person looked and saw failure another can look and see possibilities. Even we make different choices in marriage because of what we see. The difference between a person that saw failure and another that sees possibility is the word they receive. A people which receive the same information can see different things because of their thoughts. These people think differently even though received the same information because they have different values. We don't see the same thing because of our values. The things we see as we look are the information in our minds. We can program our lives to work in a particular way if we sieve the words we hear. There is the word that builds a creative mind and there is word that makes finished goods mind. Why people are not creative is because they have not seen something better in creativity.

A people that receive better words on creativity cannot see the same thing with the people that receive negative words on creativity. People within the finished goods system are corrupt and underdeveloped because what they saw made them so. It is what you see that determines your choice. Where there are options people make different choices because of what they see. There is a knowledge that makes the person that chooses option "A" to chose "A". That is why we need the right knowledge to choose right because it is the person with right knowledge that makes the right choice. Therefore, it is right to say that the word we receive determines what we see and what we see determines our choice.

The system of the creative world makes it easy for people to do right while that of finished goods makes it difficult for people to do right. The challenge of finished goods is what people with good mind face in the finished goods system. This is like the challenge creatures with lungs face in water, and in such a case they need artificial oxygen to survive. Adaptation is a prerequisite requirement for survival.

The characteristics of creativity naturally reflect on the person with a creative mindset while those of finished goods reflect on the person with finished goods' mindset. The attractive force of the value makes the characteristics of creativity to run in the veins of the person with a creative mindset and that of finished goods in the veins of people with finished goods mindset.

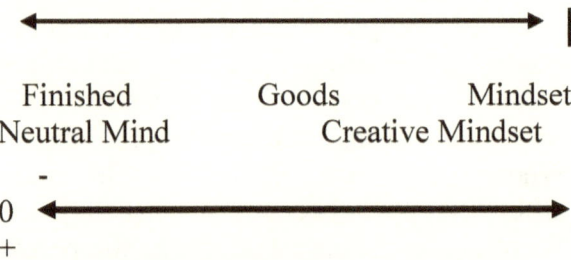

Finished   Goods   Mindset
Neutral Mind   Creative Mindset

Fig1. Graph of Development of Nations

The above illustration shows that development is progressive and the

∧∧∧

requirement for development is the creative mindset. Nations become developed when the people have positive mindset and undeveloped if negative mindset. Positive mindset is the mindset for development. Since man is progressing in knowledge the right word to use for finished goods minded nations are the developing nations. Nations are measured by their rate of development. The developmental indices are the parameters for measuring development. Development is measured by positive matrices. That is why there are the developed and the developing nations. The word underdevelopment is not often used because underdevelopment does not measure development positively.

In Walter (1972), underdevelopment is not the absence of development because every people have developed in one way or another and to a greater or lesser extent. Underdevelopment makes sense only as a means of comparing levels of development. It is very much tied to the fact that human social development has been uneven and from a strictly economic view point some human groups have advanced further by producing more and becoming wealthier.

Nations are classed as developed and developing nations according to their indices of development. The countries with high indices of development are higher in the developmental graph while those with low level of development are lower. This is why the place of creative minded nations is higher than that of finished goods. The graph below depicts the level of development with respect to creativity.

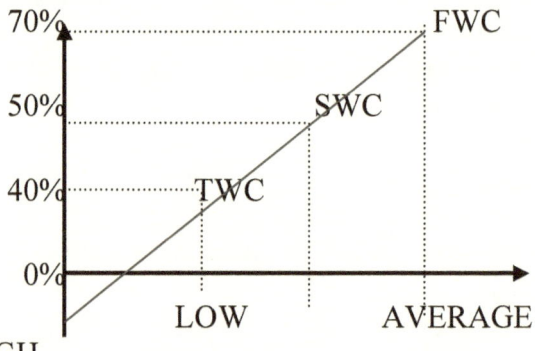

Figure2. Graph of Creative level of Nations
FWC= First World Countries, SWC= Second World Countries and TWC= Third World Countries.

The development of a country is achieved by increased creativity. The First Worlds are up in the creative graph because their level of creativity is high. Second Worlds are in the middle because their level of creativity is in the average while the Third Worlds are low in the creative graph because their level of creativity is low. Third World Countries are poor because their level of creativity is poor. Therefore, to make a rich and developed nation our creative nature as a

^^^

nation must be high. Nigerian must have creative mindset to make a better nation.

S/N	COUNTRIES	% OF VALUE ON CREATIVITY	CREATIVE LEVEL
1	FIRST WORLD	70% AND ABOVE	HIGH
2	SECOND WORLD	50% - 60%	AVERAGE
3	THIRD WORLD	LESS THAN 40%	LOW

Table 1: Shows the Creative level of First, Second and Third World Countries

DEVELOPMENTAL CONDITIONS

A nation is a body and as a body it needs to be in a given system to make development. A good example of a system that can be used to explain the state of a nation is a balloon. The balloon is an interesting phenomenon. It can shrink and expand due to a number of factors. The pumping of air is necessary for the expansion of a balloon in a confined system, and lack of leakage is the condition for enlargement. It is the leakage of air that makes the balloon that is pumped to shrink.

The development of a nation can be likened to the blowing of a balloon. The scope of government is its field of influence. The geopolitical zones experience development in a confined state. Our system should be able to regulate the exchanges between the zones because a leakage can underdeveloped the people by making the effort of government ineffective. There should be a legal medium of exchange.

Leakages result in wastage. The act of leakages under develops a nation. Some of the leakages that under develop nations so much is invested are unprofessionalism, crisis and inability to regulate activities. These and it likes do not develop a nation. Illegal transactions are not for the good of the country because they are channel for leakages.

Some of the conditions for national development are Regulation, Human Capital Development and Peace.

Regulation

A door is used to regulate movement in and out of a house. Properties in the house are secured by the door. A house without a door is like a country without security. People loot the valuable in the house because it has no door. That is why every insecure house is empty and dirty. Nothing good found in it

∧∧∧

because there is no regulation of movements.

The importance of a door cannot be over emphasized. The door secures, regulates, protects, preserves, and checks movement into in and out of the house. That is why the house without a quality door is in danger. In the same way, the nation without quality security manning its borders is in danger. We don't control what we do not regulate. There are many productive activities that do not benefit the country as they should because the system does not regulate them. The worst happens when the borders are porous. If we cannot control the activities in our borders we cannot regulate migrations.

The enemies of a country operate at its weak zones. The areas of weakness are the enemy's strength. Those areas of weakness can be likened to the place of leakage in a balloon. These areas of weakness are points where the nation loses out its investments. Just as the air pumped into balloon is lost through these areas of leakage so does a nation lose out their investment through these zones of weakness?

The zones of weakness are the underdeveloped areas. Investment brings development and exploitation brings underdevelopment. Illegal transactions are mostly within the zones of weakness. Many a time fuel tankers are diverted to other countries through the zones of weakness. The activities of Boko Haram are difficult to control because they operate at the zones of weakness. This illegal body uses the advantage of weak zones to establish their strongholds in parts of the country.

Boko Haram (Jama'atu Ahlis Sunna Lidda'awati Wal-Jahad) can be seen as a body of extremists involved in a political - religious movement out to crush any obstacle on their way. Their indent activities are with the object of establishing a government through the weak zones of the country. That is why Nigeria's territories need to be strongly guarded to ensure internal security. To guarantee effective security, both the external and internal aspects need to re-inforce each other. There is no country that combats internal insecurity with a porous border because a porous border is like a leaking balloon.

A review of the country's immigration law is necessary for the more effective regulation of the activities in the borders. The country whose borders are porous might not develop regardless of the degree of investment. If infusing of air does not develop a balloon with a leakage then nation with porous borders cannot make meaningful development. Just as it is wasteful furnishing a room without a door so it is futile investing in porous borders.

∧∧∧

Investors create employment, increase production, boost the economy and bring development. Investors are the live wire of a nation. Growth begins by investment. Even the value of Naira appreciates by investment. We must invest on our land to experience real development. We seek for investors but the truth is that we do to ourselves what we want people to do to us. Who will invest in our land when we are afraid to do so? Charity begins at home. Nations treat us as we treat ourselves. The path we present is the path they follow.

Some of the factors to consider for investment are:
- The people.
- Basic Amenities and Infrastructure
- Raw Materials
- Government Policies

These are things to consider because foreign investors are out to make profit. Just as we want their investment to profit us so they want to make gains through their investments. The security of their business is paramount. No one make an investment to lose but make profit.

Nations experience social-economic growth when her borders are difficult to penetrate by exploiters and easier to be accessed by genuine developers. You don't open doors for thieves. Why the door was made is to prevent thieves from entering. Doors are open for people with good intention. That is why nations that want to grow their economy regulate the entrance of people through their border.

To grow our economy demands we have the mindset of investing in our country. There is no need of opening the borders to those who have nothing to offer the nation. This is because it smacks of insanity to invest in a nation with porous borders and expect it to grow. The cross – border activities need to be properly regulated for national growth.

A room sprayed with insecticide, for instance, flit produces the required result only when its doors and windows are closed. The mosquitoes in the room die because the diffusion from the spray has saturated the room. Even in boiling, impurity increases the boiling point and a covered pot boils faster than the uncovered one because of the escape of molecules of water in the uncovered pot.

Some of the instabilities the country experienced come because what was budgeted for the country has been diverted. A porous country that has a rich endowment is seen as the land for miscreants. These unscrupulous elements exist because of the porosity. A country is said to be secured only when the activities in her borders are regulated. The activities at the borders determine the level of security. Therefore, let us regulate the activities in our borders to grow our economy.

Human Capital Development

Capacity building is essential for the development of nations. Uneducated minds retard development. Education is the indispensable thing parents can give to their children. We become assets through development. Inadequate training can make children become miscreants and constitutes nuisance in the society. Human Capital Development is the development for profit.

Human resources are agents for socio – economic and political development of any country while the other resources are the tools needed for the development. There is no development without the factor of human resources. Creative ability needs to be activated to bring development because creativity makes the trend that is followed while knowledge keys one into it. To become relevance in the world demand we acquire knowledge of the creativity for the time.

The government that invests in human capital development has the capacity to overcome the challenges of unemployment because the developed minds can create relevant things of high demand so lead to the exportation of finished goods and the importation of unrefined resources. We need to develop our creative abilities because many traditional skills have become obsolete.

Some of the industries in Nigeria have closed because the demand for product has declined due to the inability of making the product meet the demand of changing world. Of course, one who does not update his knowledge soon becomes obsolete in the face of rapidity of changes in the world. Therefore, in order to have a stable economy, nations must constantly invest in her people so as to meet the demands of the changing world.

Peace
The enabling environment for development is peace. Development is experienced when there is peace and underdevelopment where there is crisis. The place of peace in nation building cannot be disregard because without it there is no development. No sane person invests his hard earned money in a turbulent environment. That is why a re – orientation of the value is necessary. People should be able to differentiate between the wrong and the right. Sound morals need to be taught in our institutions. The churches and mosques have to play major role in inculcating morals. Nigeria as a country has majority of her citizen belonging to either of

the religious groups. How we react or respond to faith depend on what was taught.

An enabling environment is an engine room for growth. Imagine what happens in drought! The effect of drought shows that it is easy to destroy than build. Even if the soil is fertile the growth will be limited. Drought makes the farmer to be at a lost, many crops die up in the process, some remain stunted while those with deep roots somehow survive. Drought is a destroyer. When we study the courses of drought we would appreciate why it is necessary to regulate activities in our borders. There is need to protect our environment from aggression.

CHAPTER SEVEN
CORRUPTION

Oxford Advanced Learner's Dictionary 7th Edition defined corruption as the act or effect of making something change from moral to immoral standard of behavior. From the above definition we can say that corruption is decay in the system. Corruption is a compromise of a standard in order to achieve cheap personal gains. Another word for corruption is stain, dirty or adulteration. The work of a stain is synonymous the effect of corruption. The word 'corruption' is encompassing; stealing, embezzlement, forgery, bribe, and cheating are components of corruption, therefore, whatever that is not moral in the system is a corruption.

It is corruption that limits development especially in the developing countries. Although, the developed world have not attained the development envisaged, the rate of corruption in developed countries is low compared to that of the developed worlds. Whichever the direction of the argument, a nation cannot become developed where corruption subdues development. Developed countries attain their height of development because they were able to control the rate of corruption to the minimal level. Corruption and underdevelopment are inversely

∧∧∧

proportional to one another. It is corruption and underdevelopment work together. Where there is corruption there is underdevelopment.

It is the act of corruption that underdevelops a nation. For instance, a stain can reduce the cleanliness of a white cloth from 100% clean to about 30%. This work of the stain has undervalued the clean white cloth. Corruption devalues (under develops) a nation. It is corruption that erodes hard work and integrity. When a system is corrupt the benefit of governance will not be seen in the land and in the life of the citizenry.

Former Nigerian president, Chief Olusegun Obasenjo once said in an interview that, 'in the past, people blessed the people that own cars because they believed that they have worked hard but now people curse them because they believe they might have stolen public money'. The new perception is because the value of integrity and hard work is no longer there. He also said that in the past the families of those who do bad things were ostracized but now a thief because he has money would be the first people will like to give their daughters for marriage.

CAUSES OF CORRUPTION
Everyone needs a better world but how many can make things better! We imagined a better country, a better society and a better

place without imagining a better man. If Nigeria is likened to Nigerians, how can we make our environment better without changing our lives for good?

The problem of Nigeria begins with Nigerians. We are the nation and the nation is us. Our live manifest the state of the nation; therefore, if our lives are better, then the nation will be better. A better nation begins from us. The journey for a better Nigeria begins by how we make our lives better. If I make my world better, you make your world better and everybody makes his world better Nigeria will be a better place.

The problem is neither strictly with the leaders nor followers but Nigerians. No person or group of persons is the problem of Nigeria because the man with influence is the person with the masses. The power of a leader is with the masses. It is the man that has the masses that has the power. No leader can rule without the masses. If Nigeria is a population of more than 160 million people is even a worst deception to think that the problem is caused by an individual because the mindset of the people is the product of the value. One who attacks an individual leaves the main problem for shadow.

The problem of the nation is her value – finished goods. There are different options before us but what we choose is the problem. The people are even far from the problem because to deal with the problem

∧∧∧

we have to begin with the value. This value deals with the system and mindset. It is the value system that is the problem because Nigerians will not have the mindset of finished goods without the value system (finished goods system).

Values system is the ground for operation. We are in a systemic world. The world is governed by laws and principles. Therefore, everything we do live by principles. Scientists speak of the laws of nature, gravitation, thermodynamics and so forth. It is these laws that make the events of life constant. Laws are observable, measurable, and repeatable because they do not change. It is the law that controls people's action. Thus, if the system is good, bad people will find it difficult to operate and if the system is bad, good people will find it difficult to operate. The ground is made fertile for those that work in the system just as crops grow well in their soil.

The working mechanism of a system is not in a person it is rather in the value system of the place. Good leadership and bad system are opposites. Accident results when the good and bad meet. There will be a clash when somebody is not working in line with the tenets of the system. That is why a good leader will not be effective in a bad system and a bad leader cannot achieve his bad ambitions in a good system. Therefore, if there are problems in the country, it is not completely from the leader but the system. Our leaders are not our problems, the problem of the nation is the value system.

Governance is a trust. It takes the expression of love for the people to willingly obey. People find it difficult to obey the law when the system is not the spirit of the law. Constitution deals with 'Will and Testament'. Somebody must be willing to testify. One has to receive the word of the constitution to do them. If the people find it difficult to obey, then it means that what is written is not the system of the country. It is difficult to obey a constitutional law that is not the system of the country.

If a system is divinely designed for operation, there is nobody who works against a system that goes unpunished. If a system is bad good people who worked against the bad system will receive an undeserved punishment. That is why people hardly expose wrong doers in a finished goods system because those who have tried were victimized for their actions. Somebody with a good mind can compromise as a result of the negative influence of the system.

Fighting corruption in a corrupt system is like washing dirty cloth in dirty water. Anti graft bodies will not work better in a corrupt system. These regulatory bodies compromise standards because of the

∧∧∧

system. When the soil is not fertile the plant will not grow well. It takes a fertile soil to make a good plant. Even members of security agents will not find it difficult to enforce laws and order in a creative system. This is because the system has already made the environment not conducive for corrupt minds. Fighting corruption is easy in creative system. It is in a corrupt system that people finds it difficult to fight corruption.

Systemic change is inevitable in the pursuit for better Nigeria. Many innovative Nigerians who hardly survive in the country thrive in the developed world because of the congenial system of those nations. This class of people thrives because there is a system that makes them succeed in their goods works. The system that brings out the innate potential of man is the creative one. Finished goods system does not bring out man's innate potential and that's why people live fake lives to succeed.

People easily thrive in what they do in a credible system. The fish thrives in water. The terrestrial and aquatic animals do not operate in the same system. Since the ground for operation is the system, permanent solution to the problem will only come as we deal with the root of the problem because the mindset of people is dependent on the value system of the nation.

Nigerians

The problems of Nigeria are Nigerians. There is no nation in the world that can stop the development of Nigeria than Nigerians. If there is problem, then the mindset of the people is the problem. When the mind is corrupt and underdeveloped the nation will be corrupt and underdeveloped. It is the information one receives that he become. For instance, a medical doctor is one who received medical words. There is nobody that is born a medical doctor. The mind of a child at birth is tabula rasa (empty). It is the word received that the child becomes. Nobody becomes what he did not receive. Somebody who did not receive medical word cannot become a medical doctor. What makes you are the words you receive? People are corrupt not because they are born corrupt but because of the words of corruption they received. The relationship between you and the word you receive is that the word you receive is you.

Word creates world. What you are is not different from the word you receive. The word you receive yesteryear is what you are today and the word you are receiving today is what you will become tomorrow. Tell me the words you receive and I will tell you who you are! Tell me the value of a nation and I will tell you what the nation is like! There is the world of music, the world of engineering, the world of medicine, the world of science, the world of politics, etc. The world you find yourself is the product of the word received. It is the word received that determines who you are.

Word when heard creates thoughts in your mind. The reaction of a word in your mind is the positive and negative thoughts. These thoughts are like chemical molecules that can be bound to produce a compound. Thoughts are invisible particles that bombard our minds. A single word can create millions of thoughts/time. These thoughts created can be received or rejected. The thoughts that are received bounds to produce a mindset. The mindset is an individual. Why people are different is because they have different mindsets. One is not different from his mindset. Therefore, your mindset is you.

The summary of the process is: Words create thoughts, the thoughts received bound to form a mindset. Somebody's personality is his mindset. The state of Nigeria is what we choose. Nigeria is corrupt and underdeveloped because we choose the word that makes us corrupt and underdeveloped. It is not an individual that chose it for us, we chose it by ourselves. One who has access to information can access both good and bad information. We have access to both information but we decided to choose finished goods because we are ignorant of its consequences. It is ignorance that makes us think that finished goods will be for our good. Now we have the light as it were, let us change our perspectives fo the good of our society.

Value System
The root of Nigeria problem is corrupt knowledge. One cannot do anything without a word. The information we hear and do are the very information that makes us. The nation's problem is internal and not external. We leave the real problem and fight shadows when we are superficial. It is important we look inwards in finding lasting solutions to our problems. Lack of formal education, unemployment, poverty, corruption and underdevelopment are not Nigeria's major problems. In fact, we have so many educated people who are corrupt so lack of formal education is not the problem. It is not poverty either because so many rich people are corrupt. The problem is not corruption because there is something that caused corruption.

The result of one's effort is seen in the output. The effort of the governance is seen in the governed; that of the teacher is seen on the student and the value system of a nation is seen on the mind – set of the people. The mind – set reflects the value inculcated. Somebody cannot have the wrong mindset and not corrupt. People are corrupt because their minds are corrupt. Inability to deal with the root cause of the problem is why our efforts in salvaging the country from corruption and underdevelopment have not yielded result. The aforementioned are the results of the problem because the nation cannot experience corruption if the people received not corrupt knowledge.

Corrupt knowledge when received gives birth to corrupt thoughts which create corrupt mindset that makes one corrupt. It is the reaction of corrupt knowledge with our minds that produces poverty, corruption, poor quality education, underdevelopment etc. Somebody is corrupt when his mind is programmed with the information that corrupts. Therefore, the best way to solve corruption problems is to deal with the corrupt information that creates the system which gives the value.

Our actions and reactions in life are based on what we hear. Even terrorism is based on belief. It is the word we receive that forms our faith. Indeed that constitutes our belief. Knowledge and mindset work together. It is the word received that forms our mindset. We meditate on a particular word so that we can have the mindset to do the word. One who wants good things guides his mind from bad things. It is corrupt words that make people corrupt. We are not everything because we don't receive every word. It is the word we receive that we become. The person that guides his mind from corrupt words cannot be corrupt. Many a time it is ignorance that makes people to venture into things that can destroy them.

The word of finished goods is the cause of corruption. This is because it has the capacity to cause greed. When the finished goods' reacts on our mind what is produced are corruption and underdevelopment. The relationship between finished goods and corruption is that corruption is the product of finished goods. When the mind is filled with falsehood one cannot but live falsely. Corruption thrives because people work to get the best finished goods to satisfy their insatiable needs.

SOLUTIONS TO CORRUPTION

We deal with information on finished goods by giving better information on creativity. For instance, a rejected stone becomes a precious stone by the information that gives it value. People are attracted to something by the information they have about it. That is why people fight to have a portion on the land where crude oil is discovered. Perhaps, nobody wanted that land before crude oil was discovered. The value of crude oil is simply what attracts people to the rejected land.

∧∧∧

We invest our money for a value. It takes the value of something for people to buy the product. People spend their money, time, talent and resources on something with value and the information given on that thing is its value. Information is the price tag of anything. The quality of information on Mr A is what makes Mr A receive $10,000,000 annually and Mr B $100 annually. Mr B might be better than Mr A but the value of Mr A is higher because of the information available on him.

People venture into say, business because of the information on it. Although, the value of gold is high, nobody will buy gold with high amount without positive information on it. Our values are revealed in our behaviors, moralities, standards, permits, priorities, the things we celebrate, accept and reject. Values form the foundation of nations and profoundly shape the lives and daily experiences of their citizens.

If man is a product of a word, to change a person will require a change in the words he receives. It is not enough to empower people to live independently rather it is enough to change their mindset. One whose mindset is dependent cannot live independently even after several empowerments. If you can make somebody to receive new words you can change the person. Everybody is subject to change and if one can receive new words then that person can change. People do not change when they have not received words better than the word that had given them the unproductive mindset. It is the better words received that commands change.

The solution to corruption and underdevelopment is the creative system. A system can be formed by words and action. Just as a builder can build and rebuild a house so we can create and recreate a system. What it takes to create a system is its channel. If the channel is created, the system will have no choice than flow. As water flows through it channel so does a system flows through it channel. Nigerians can operate in a creative system only when we create the channel.

We need a more powerful word to change the word on corruption. People become corrupt because the value placed on finished goods is higher than the value of creativity. We need to present a better value to make a better Nigeria. The system can be creative when we present better information on creativity over finished goods. When better information on creativity is given people will naturally be creative without persuasion because there is nobody that will like to be at the losing end. It is the winning team that attracts minds.

Issues are handled based on the way we value them. People put their minds on issues with higher value. For instance, if governance is made more lucrative, people will have no other choice than bury their potentialities in the world of politics. That is why people leave one thing for another when what was not valued becomes valued. The system is corrupt because there is value on finished goods over creativity. When the finished goods' minds are more valued than the creative minds people will become finished goods minded irrespective of the positive things you think and say about creativity.

To reject a value means to accept another value. We are programmed and reprogrammed by the type of information received. Behaviorists have come to terms that human behavior can be learned and unlearned. Information molds the inward man and the result of the molding is transformation. Internal formation (information) brings external reformation (transformation). To change a man externally will first require that the person is changed internally. People are made by the word they receive.

Man does not solve a problem by using the same information that created the problem. The information that solves a problem is opposite of the one that created the problem. Positive value is always used to solve negative problems. For instance, $-1 + 1 = 0$. The aforementioned mathematical expression proves that one who knows the problem can find the solution because the opposite could be the solution.

We need the information that is directly opposite finished goods to solve the finished goods problems. To combat corruption and underdevelopment requires we break away from the information that forms corruption in our minds. The mindset of the people will not change when the information that caused the mindset is not changed. Attacking this value or information is uprooting the problem from its root.

There is a difference between the words "uproot" and "cut down". When we cut down we solve temporal problems but when we uproot we solve permanent problems. Killing people believed to be corrupt can only bring temporal solution but a change of value system shall bring permanent solution to corruption. People talk about revolution that almost collapsed the nation in 1966 as the solution to the country's problems. They forget the fact that what appears to work in other nations might not work in Nigeria and the very thing our fathers did is the actual thing we will do in the same system. As long as the grass in the field is not uprooted it will always bud its kind.

A different species of grass in the field can only thrive by a total overhaul. This overhauling might require a particular type of soil for a given plant. There are plants

∧∧∧

that are not cultivated in sandy soil. The right type of soil is necessary for every plant. The tiling of ground enables the plant to grow. When the soil is not cultivated the main plant will find it difficult to thrive. It is the tilling of the soil that makes it good for agriculture. The system of making the soil good for the right plant to grow is the same system that is applied in making a better nation.

For a better nation to emerge, the system must be fertile for creativity. This can be done by forming a creative system. A creative system should be watered and nurtured with creative values. Creative information is what we need to make a creative system. These can be seen by recognizing and appreciating creative minds far above the finished goods mindset.

In a creative environment the nation will be more of producers than consumers because people will apply innovation in their daily activities. The brain will be active and the spirit will be high as one is poised to make things better. Innovation is the way forward because it will meet consumers' need. That is what it takes for a hitherto underdeveloped economy to buy its way into the global market.

We need to form a creative system for people to leave the mindset of finished goods because the mind cannot leave a value until its system is altered. A system creates and transfers value, that is why a chair can be called a throne. The power of a system will make what is not valuable to become valued. In fact, the neglected rock can become the most valuable in a change of system.

Change is nothing more than transferring value, and whatever that does not accept change becomes extinct because everything on earth is subject to it. To experience a positive change as a nation demands that creativity becomes our value. Though it may seem difficult because it is difficult to accept change but if we can decide to accept change, the true Nigeria is possible.

Our ability to accept change will make things to change around us. We cannot experience change if our mindset does not change. This is because the mindset is the battle that must be won for things to change. It is what differentiates a normal human being from the madman, and until we overcome it by redefining our value, nothing will change. Just as the person who is absent-minded can hear without listening, look and not see so does the program initiated to change the mindset which does not affect the system will yield no result!

The mindset of finished goods is reprogrammed in the creative system because the human mind can be reprogrammed by the value system.

∧∧∧

Therefore, what serves as our value as children is expected to change as we grow? Unchanged value makes an adult childish. Nigeria is now of age, so, it is expected that Nigerians should grow above child's mentality because the mindset of finished goods (consumers) is the mindset of children. That is why they can take everything into their mouth and even refuse one a little of the much he gave them.

The word "developing" can be used as an expression for an immature mind. This is the place for children. It takes maturity to fully develop because developed nations are matured nations. It is the nation that is fully grown that is developed. Lack of basic requirement for development is the reason for underdevelopment. A nation that is underdeveloped can be said to experience poor growth. Nigeria will develop fast if she receives balanced requirement for development at right ratio.

A creative mindset will make us have something to offer the nation but the finished goods mindset will make us have nothing to offer the nation, therefore, we have to change from the mentality of keeping to ourselves so that our country can live. Man's debt is to make his environment better. This means that we should begin to ameliorate our environment to clear the debts of corruption and underdevelopment.

The principle that governs a nation is the system. Every government is run on a system. If we can change from the system that underdeveloped us, there will be nothing that can stop Nigeria from attaining its expected height of development. A change of system is the only way out of corruption and underdevelopment.

Inordinate values should not be placed on goods at the expense of creativity because the people whose value is creativity naturally own the secondary product - finished goods. Nigeria can form a creative system by acknowledging and rewarding creative achievers at the expense of finished goods minded people. Given prominence to base on numbers of houses, cars and the amount of money in bank accounts can only increase greed but rewarding creative achievers at the expense of the finished goods achievers will naturally showcase creative scenario. This system will project our rich cultural heritage, arts and indigenous technology.

CHAPTER EIGHT
GOOD GOVERNANCE

Oxford Advanced Learner's Dictionary 7th Edition defined government as a group of people responsible for controlling a country or state. The essence of government is the people and it is institutionalized to establish order. A society without law and government is bound to live in Chaos. Laws enforce and protect the standards by which the country operates. Government is a body institutionalized for the people. Good governance is all about the good of the people. The dividends of democracy are delivered through good governance.

International Monetary Fund (IMF) declared in 1996 that promoting good governance in all it aspect, including by ensuring the rule of law, improving the efficiency and accountability of the public sector and tackling corruption, as essential elements of a framework within which economies can prosper. The IMF feels that corruption within economies is caused by the ineffective governance of the economy, either too much regulation or too little regulation.

According to the United Nations (UN), good governance has eight characteristics.
1. Consensus Oriented
2. Participatory
3. Rule of Law
4. Effective and Efficient
5. Accountable
6. Transparent
7. Responsible
8. Equitable and Inclusive

Good governance is an indeterminate term used in international development literatures to describe how public institutions conduct public affairs and manage public resources. The concept of good governance centers on the responsibility of governments and governing bodies to meet the needs of the masses as opposed to select groups in society.

In international affairs, analysis of good governance can be considered along the following subheadings:
1. Between Government and Markets
2. Between Government and Citizens
3. Between Government and the Private or Voluntary Sectors
4. Between Elected and Appointed Officials

Again, to refer to President Obama's speech, what Africa needs is not more strong men, but more strong democratic institutions that will stand the test of time. Without good governance no amount of oil, no amount of

∧∧∧

aid, no amount of effort can guarantee Nigeria's success. But with good governance, nothing can stop Nigeria (Wikipedia).

The working of a nation is not in a person it is rather realizable in the system. In a democratic environment like Nigeria, political stability can be achieved through efficient rule of law, strong institutions rather than strong individuals, a responsive and effective bureaucracy and conducive investment climate. A strong person cannot solve the nation's challenges but a democratic institution that is creative in nature can. Nigerians are not wild life that needs strong hands, Nigerians are rational beings; therefore, are stable if given the opportunity to choose. It is crude and uncivilized to maltreat people. Man is an intelligent being therefore knows what is good for him.

If what we need even as attest by the outside world is more strong democratic institutions then it means that government is not a person or a group of persons but a system. The group of people who are responsible for controlling a country or a state are part of a people therefore are not enough to make a government because government is the people. It takes follower-ship and leadership to make a government. Neither or either of them there is no government.

Leaders are chosen to establish a government. This means that every dispensation of leadership forms a new government. The emergence of a leader is the emergence of a government. A leader is a bridge builder. A leader is expected to take the people from where they are to where they want to be. The gap between the rich and the poor can be bridged by a leader. It is in a society where there is no leader that there is survival of the fittest. The rich get richer and the poor poorer in a survival of the fittest because where there is survival of the fittest it will take the strong to live.

Government is formed to accommodate both the weak and strong. Leadership deals with the ability to organize and harmonize people. It is an error when a leader gets richer and his followers get poorer. This is because the life of a leader is directly proportional to the life of his followers. Great kings are those with great followers. The relationship between the follower and the leader in a good system is one.

∧∧∧

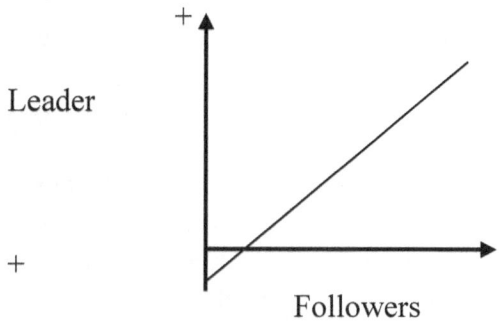

Leader

+

Followers

Fig3. Graph of leader and followers in good system

Leader = K of Followers

K = Leader/Followers = 1

If they are one then a leader is not appointed or elected to impoverish the people because what is good for the leader is good for the followers. The life of a leader should reflect in his followers. Leadership is a sacrifice, therefore one should be able to sacrifice to be a true leader. Somebody who makes people work on a goal is a leader. People go their different ways where there is no leader. A people without a leader are like sheep without a shepherd.

The character of a leader demands charisma because it takes authority and power to govern. Authority has to do with responsibility while power deals with ability. Both authority and power must balance for a government to succeed. A good leader must have the will power to govern. He must be able to make the people work in a particular direction. That means a leader can also be seen as the one who initiates change. For instance, a leader could make a people change from finished goods to creative mindset.

Government is a change and systemic change is what the nation needs. The platform for good governance is the need of the people. If the people are tired of corruption and underdevelopment then it means the nation needs a creative system. Governance is rendering service to the people. It is the responsibility of the leader to make the lives of the people better. The need of the people comes first in governance because without the people there are no leaders.

A leader visualizes the government he wants and makes the people work therein. It is the responsibility of the leader to create an environment that will enable the people to do the task he wants. This can be achieved by making the governed belief him. There is need for proper motivation to follow a dedicated leader.

Some of the working conditions that can make the follower to follow are;

a.   Access to Human Physiological Needs

b.   Equity and Justice

c.   Acknowledgment   and Encouragement

d.   Vision

Good governance is all about service to the people. That which meets the need of the masses is good governance. The government that is for the good of the people is the government of the people, by the people and for the people.

Access to Human Physiological Needs

The best way to win the mind of a child is to meet his needs. Basic amenities are direct parameters for measuring development but the indirect and the most essential parameter is the basic needs of the people. One of the responsibilities of government is the provision of basic amenities to people. Basic amenities include water, electricity, sanitary facilities, housing, road etc. These amenities create good access to human's basic needs.

Access to man's basic needs might create no room for excessive accumulation of wealth. The fear of poverty is the cause of the excessive accumulation of wealth. That is why people can exploit their country. This mindset is created because of poor accessibility to human physiological needs. In other words, poverty mentality makes the minds to remain corrupt even after the basic needs have been met. Inability to meet human physiological needs is poverty. Thus, the mentality of keeping to oneself can be erased when the human physiological needs are made affordable to all and sundry.

This loop-hole was created because human physiological needs are not guaranteed. And since the physiological need is taking as a survival, the need to have them can make people corrupt because they are required to sustain life. Do's and don'ts are not easily observed when one cannot solve his physiological needs. People are stable when they live beyond the thoughts of physiological needs.

Food, water, shelter, education and health care are essential for the realization of the goals of policies. There might be no policy that matters more to a hungry man besides food. What controls the mind of a hungry person is food. Food overrules developmental thoughts in his mind because it is a basic need. Even a sick person who has no access to health care does not think anything apart from his health. People don't follow policies that do not meet their basic need.

One of the effects of poverty is that it makes one slave to those things people have legitimate rights to. Access to basic needs and amenities makes one to have a wide range of thought but poor access narrows one's thought to the basic needs. People lack direction when they live below human's physiological needs. Man is limited by the

∧∧∧

level of his thought; hence, to think beyond limitation, basic needs and amenities have to be made accessible for the people.

Maslow's theory of human needs suggests that the most basic level of needs must be met before the individual will strongly desire (or focus motivation upon) the secondary or higher level needs. He classified hierarchy of human needs as;

1. Physiological needs
2. Safety needs
3. Love and Belonging
4. Esteem
5. Self-actualization
6. Self-transcendence

In the hierarchy, Maslow placed priority on the physiological needs. According to him, "for the most part, physiological needs are obvious – they are the literal requirement for human survival. If these requirements are not met, the human body simply cannot continue to function. Air, water and food are metabolic requirements for survival in all animals, including humans. Cloths and shelter provide necessary protection from elements" (Maslow's hierarchy of needs).

Equity and Justice

Equal representation of people with different backgrounds is necessary for development. In a complex nation like Nigeria the interest of each zone has to be considered for people to work together. Structural adjustment technique is needed to establish the equilibrium for all round development. This simple mathematical permutation can effect some changes in the system.

Man naturally wants to be found in a place where his effort can be acknowledge and rewarded. Lack of acknowledgment of values, usefulness and productivity can make people change their preferences - say from good to bad. Brains are drained when there is no equity and justice. When polished ideas for development are not utilized one will have no choice than go to places his ideas are valued. There is no justice in a case where all are not equal. Perhaps, how can there be justice when some organs are made superior to others?

Inequality has made people to neglect their fields of strength in their choice of careers as well make the desire to offer the nation something no meaning. That is why many things which impede development happen as people strive to work in the preferred sectors. What ordinarily would have been work has virtually turned to a rat race even as survival of the fittest has enveloped the minds of those who desire socio-economic growth of the country.

Structural imbalance has made people to occupy wrong positions, and the more people move away from their fields of strength the more corrupt, lustful, less useful and unproductive they become. People make things worse when they lack the capacity to make them better. Love is built in the field while lust is built outside the field. To work for the development of the nation will demand that people work in their fields of strength. This is because the love for the things they do shall cause them to give for the development of the nation.

Fig.11. An illustration of events within and outside fields of strengtl

When people leave their field of strength, they give nothing because they have nothing to give. Even a professor of Education who is not talented in the field might not make much impart in teaching no matter how much he studies to teach because his knowledge will be limited to the known. The person cannot go beyond what he/she read (studied), heard, and saw others do. People find it difficult to even do the jobs they are paid to do when their jobs are not their hobbies. Training can develop a talented teacher and can also make one who is not naturally empowered in the field to be seen as a gifted teacher.

Every human being has the place of his best. Just as our faces differ so our potentials. A monkey will always be a monkey. There is no amount of training that can make a monkey human being. The best so far achieved was to make a monkey behave like a human being. If the environment cannot change the nature of a monkey then it means that heredity and environment have their boundaries. There is a place for the two and both are required for total development of man's well being.

Productivity is hindered when we are not in our specialty. What people need to enhance production is the right place. People might not value the most talented player until he displays his skill in the pitch. True success is not just a product of hard work and struggles but the work in one's field of strengths.

Man's satisfaction or fulfillment comes by working in his field of strength. The person who is destined to be in a place but finds himself in another place will not have rest until he reaches his destination. Even trains are made to move on the rail and not on water like ship or on road like a car. To be productive demands that people should work in areas that enhance the fulfillment of their purpose in life because a purposeful mind is an innovative mind.

Hard Work - Purpose = Activities

In the areas of strength, less than 50% effort is required to make more than 50% production while outside the fields, more than 50% effort is required to make up to 50% production. Activity is not synonymous with productivity; therefore, we need to be result oriented to be productive.

Productivity = Hard Work + Purpose

Lack of creative mindset has made many well educated, hardworking personnel with wealth of experience work without innovations. Can we solve the puzzle in which an uneducated person can own companies that employ the best brains in relevant fields while the educated may not be able to do so? Why is it that some people with great knowledge cannot create something from which others can acquire knowledge?

One may acquire all the certificates in mechanical engineering but has not invented the smallest and simplest thing in the field; has a good knowledge of music, yet cannot produce an album that transforms life. The most qualified yet cannot go beyond the knowledge acquired. Somebody is in a wrong field when he cannot discover the unknown. If we are not in our field of strength, the only contribution we can make beyond the known could be selfish.

Salt is made to taste like salt but the salt that tastes like sugar has lost its taste. Irrespective of how nice the microphone looks, without amplification of voice, the microphone has lost its value. Added knowledge that does not bring out values can make one the most qualified without leaving footprints in the sands of time as legacy are guaranteed by creative innovation.

If those who make discoveries did not leave their comfort zones, knowledge would not have risen to its present height. If our past heroes who brought us independence did not react, they would not have been celebrated today. It is only those who caused change to happen that are celebrated even in the grave. The person who did not confront will not conquer; thus, we must break out of our shell to reveal our values. The right place will maximize people's full potentials. To maximize people's full potential will demand that professionalism corresponds to passion.

People can creatively work in their fields of endeavors when the system is creative.

∧∧∧

Equity and justice in all fields of human endeavor are necessary to bring about development in its fullness. Somebody's field of strength may not be his field of studies. The former is independent of what we claim, therefore, we need to discover and develop it so as to bring the best. When sectors are treated equally people will have reasons to choose to work in their fields of strength and the negative mindset created about some sectors could die naturally.

Inequality inhabits growth and has the capacity to cause corruption because it can hide values. What do we expect people to do when there is no equality in the system? That is why people struggle to work in the so-called lucrative sectors. Somebody may not have interest in the growth of the country when he feels marginalized.

Acknowledgment and Encouragement
Acknowledgment and encouragement are two great motivations for any achievements. Nobody will like to invest more in a place his effort is not acknowledged. People are motivated to do more when their efforts are acknowledged and encouraged. That is what we need to make development. It is the motivation that enhances production.

One of the ways to encourage and acknowledge people to do more is recognition through awards. Presentation of awards of excellence can spur people to do more. People receive awards based on their contributions to national development. Some of the classes of honors and awards that can be conferred on Nigerians include;

1. The National Honors
2. The Nigerian National Merit Award
3. The National Productivity Merit Award
4. The Creativity Award

These honors are created to develop every sector of human endeavor so as to bring about all round development of society. One class of honor should not be seen as being superior to another because each of them has particular needs they meet. This is done to encourage dignity in labor. But whereas many Nigerians in different fields can mention the names of Nigerians with National Honors perhaps only few know the name of any Nigerian with creativity award? We must celebrate our creative minds to experience real development.

The motivation for people to work in their field is the value placed on the field. Prioritizing one over the other can make the system one sided. We need to cultivate the habit of giving these classes of honors and awards to deserving Nigerians. This is how the people can know their efforts are acknowledged and recognized.

Many things go wrong in the underdeveloped countries because greater percentage of their youths (the productive stage of human life) is not productive. How do we expect to make a better nation when the large number of the nation's work force is not productive? Joblessness becomes the order of the day when the system is not creative. It is a sign of immaturity for a sovereign state to depend on another country to solve especially her basic needs. That is why dependent independent countries remain poor despite her resources and international supports.

Excellence in performance is promoted by motivation. Somebody needs to be acknowledged and encouraged to be productive, and productivity is necessary for the development of nations. The development of a nation is dependent on the productive capacity of her people. It is productivity that leads to employment.

Organizations employ people because they want to increase production and their ability to produce more leads to more employment opportunities. Any organization that is not productive has no capacity to take in more people because employment without productivity is not profitable. Productivity is directly proportional to employability. Productivity

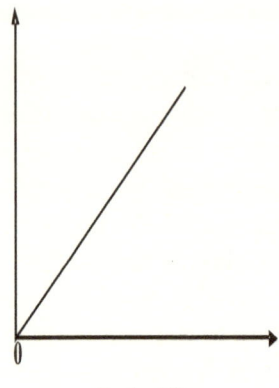

Employability

Fig.12: Graphs of Productivity against Employability

$P = KE$

$K = P/E$

Productivity = Innovation multiplied by the work done

Organization increases her employment capacity when $K>1$

Where:

P = Productivity

E = Employability

K = Constant

The promotion of staff which is not based on productivity may not enhance performance. This is one of the reasons workers become lethargic and irresponsible in executing jobs they are paid to do. Some may even demand bribe to do what they are paid for. This nonchalant attitude develops when productivity is not the watchword.

High cost of goods and difficulty in making a living will justify a high remuneration from a low productive venture. To maximize

∧∧∧

our human resources in all fields, we need to adopt a unified grading system by reconciling the disparities in salaries of workers. An equitable grading system even in salaries can enhance dignity in labor and create stability in government.

The promotion of unproductive ventures erodes productivity as well as makes the wrong trend. Promotions and salary increments should be based on value, usefulness, and productivity. An increase in production should lead to promotion and the ability to excel in one's field of endeavor should lead to an award of excellence, to motivate workers and make them more committed to their work.

It is expected that people should improve their abilities for doing things. The relevancy of one declined when he does not upgrade himself with latest knowledge. Somebody becomes outdated when he cannot update himself. The more time spent in a field the more knowledge is expected to be acquired to meet the demands of a changing world. Growth is not experienced by doing the same thing at different times because every event has its time. The demand of the changing world requires that we upgrade in whatever we do.

Man is made to effect changes. The work of man is to create and the work of the machine is to work in the programming of man.

People hardly remembers all stored in their brains because garbage in, garbage out is not the primary duty of man and since the machine cannot perform beyond what was programmed, if somebody is limited by what was taught, leaves the job the way he/she met it or cannot go beyond what is known, the person is not better than the machine.

It is better to employ the services of a machine because it has the capacity to duplicate what is needed. If the service of limiting to the known is needed, the machine should be used because it will make it; better, faster, more accurate and cheaper. A worker without innovation just needs time to be irrelevant. Man is reduced to a machine without innovation. We do not effect positively to the changing world because people have left their place as humans for an inefficient machine.

Vision

Vision is the ability to govern and the ability to govern is the ability to lead. Where there is no vision the people perish. A leader should be able to make people work for a common goal. If this is not achieved then it means there could be another light somewhere. It takes vision to lead because people do not follow the man without vision. Even insects run after light. It takes the man of light to lead the people out of darkness.

∧∧∧

The word "darkness" connotes the negative part of life. People in darkness need somebody with light to bring them to knowledge.

A group of people in the dark will need light to find their way, because in the absence of light, this people will stumble on more difficult conditions while trying to find their way. But the appearance of little light will direct everyone in that room to the source and that means the person who has the light automatically becomes the leader. Experience is not the most important quality of a leader. Somebody with wealth of experience without vision will lead the people to destruction. There is no amount of experience that can make people to follow a man without vision. The major quality of a leader is vision. Vision is the power to lead. That is what it takes to govern. The vision that is anchored on experience makes a good leader.

One's vision enables him to see beyond the limitations of others. It takes vision to see. How far somebody sees depends on his vision. There is the eyes of a leader. Leaders see the future while followers see the present. A leader is somebody who sees the future today. That is why he is not moved by the events of today because he understands that the difference between here and there is time. If the blind does not lead blind people then a leader is therefore defined as the man with a vision. It is vision that makes a leader.

Outstanding opportunities are hidden in challenges; therefore, it takes the visionary mind to see beyond the obstacles. Vision makes leaders and followers see differently. One who sees today cannot understand the person that sees the future. It is vision that makes a leader see opportunities where the followers see challenges. There difference in views is one of the reasons for distraction from followers. That is why a visionary mind needs to be strong and courageous to keep focus on his vision because his followers may not understand him in some cases since they see differently.

The resources for blessing can be a curse where there is no vision because vision is needed for effective utilization of resources. As people stumble in darkness so do people with even rich resources stumble without vision. People stumble in gross darkness when they fight and kill one another over what is meant for their good. It is lack of vision that makes a country to depend solely on the revenue from her unprocessed resources! It is equally lack of vision when there are no plans for the future! We lack vision when we desire product than the process. What is our pride when we cannot refine our petroleum? There is no vision for the country when people are sectional chauvinists or passionately canvas for their ethnic groups, forgetting that there's a bigger nation called the Federal Republic of Nigeria. It is the person who believes in Nigeria that sacrifices for the country.

If the man from Kenya can become the President of the United States, then it's enough to say that Americans place their national interest above prejudice. A man with vision is a leader. A well experienced person without a vision is only but one who recycles thoughts. What makes development is vision. We need light to move forward. Lack of vision will only destroy a leader and his followers. Therefore, to experience positive growth in all the aesthetic spheres of our national life, Nigeria needs visionary leaders and well-experienced advisers.

CHAPTER NINE
POSITIVE CHANGE

We have the land, the people and the resources. Nigeria is a nation so blessed above other nations and considering her abundant rich resources the limiting factor is the information received. The problem militating against the nation's full development is the corrupt knowledge. This gap can be closed by incorrupt information. The information devoid of corruption is what we need to tackle the problems that have bedeviled the nation.

Positive change is possible when the mind is affected positively. Our decision to do the right thing is the positive change. We might not become great without overcoming our fears. Man's limitations in life are the things he fears. If we can employ creative system in our operations most likely in year 2020 Nigeria will not just become one of the twenty world economies but a developed nation free from corruption.

What can stop the nation from achieving this goal is the finished goods' mindset. That is why making a new Nigeria demands change in the value system and mindset. As Nigerians celebrate the country's centenary there is need to redefine the value system to

^^^

build better mindset. This can be achieved by making creativity more valuable than finished goods. A transfer of value is a necessity for making the true Nigeria a reality. If the cake was our value then the making of the cake should be our new value. Creativity should be the core value. An independent nation is dependent when its core value is the finished goods. The new Nigeria needs "THE PROCESS OF MAKING MORE THAN THE PRODUCTS"

Nigerians must produce those things they need by themselves to make a developed nation because the technology for making is the secret of developed countries. Man is more valuable than every other creature because of his divine nature. Let's activate the creative abilities in us and make Nigeria a better place. If I make my environment better, you make your environment better and everybody makes his or her place better, Nigeria will not just be a better place but the envy of nations. We can make Nigeria the best place to live.

Man has creative ability because he was made to solve problems. The development of the nation lies in our hands. If we can change for good the country will change for good. The state of the nation is the product of our mindset. Man is made to recreate his world. Nations that understand the value of man's potential choose problem solving because they know it is only in so doing that man's full creative abilities are unleashed. This creative quality is what makes the nations without rich resources rule over the rich resources nations.

The finished goods' system forms the crowded zone. It is a place for the unrefined and non - renewed minds. The world of the finished goods is the world of the exterior (the life of falsehood and pretense). Life is difficult in the finished goods system because it creates no room for new ideas; as a result, the rich get richer and the poor poorer. It is the creative system that creates room for everyone. The creative system opens our minds for solution.

Growth is a response to positive change and continuation is a sign of growth. People achieve greatness by looking into the future. Thus, we must continue from where our predecessors stopped to reach the top. Developed Countries make tree – like investments while the underdeveloped nations invest in grains, and that's why they always start all over. Nigerians must have creative mindsets to transform the country for good. Creativity is what the nation needs to enjoy good governance. Hard work, Peace and Unity are products of creative system.

This book sets out to give information required to reprogram the minds of Nigerians to make for a better society. The

ᴧᴧᴧ

nugget of information concentrates on the re – orientation of the value system and mindset of the people. The mindset and the system will change only when the value is changed. Therefore, holistic overhaul of the status quo will transform the country because the system and mindset of today are products of the values sowed yesterday. A good value sown today shall better the future of the country even if the finished goods underscore the countries ultimate mandates.

Finally, the making of a new Nigeria requires creative minds. It is the reprogramming of our finished goods minds that will transform the country and the nations of Africa at large. Creativity, when imbibed will not only transform the country but will also bring about a true Nigeria. Africa and the less developed countries of the world need a creative system. The value (creativity) is what less developed nations of the world need for development. Systemic change is the panacea for African development.

BIBLIOGRAPHY

Asuquo, P.N. (2009). Basic counseling principles and procedures for teachers. Calabar. University of Calabar Press.

Denga, D. I. (2009). Special Education and special counseling services for primary and junior secondary school in Nigeria. Calabar. Rapid educational publisher limited.

Jhingan, M. L., 2008. The Economics of Development and Planning. 39th edition, Vrinda Publications Ltd.

Munroe, M. 2006. Kingdom Principles. Destiny Image Publisher Inc. Shippenburg

Obasi C., 2008. Human Capital Development. The Panacea for Organizational Growth. Online publication.

Omebe, S. E. (2014). Guidance and Counseling: Panacea for National Development. 3rd inaugural Lecture, Ebonyi State University, Abakaliki.

Shokunbi, L. (1999). "Science, technology and Nigeria's Tomorrow": The Guardian Wednesday 21st April.

Udida, L. A. (2010). Issues in National Policy on Education in Nigeria. Calabar: University of Calabar Press.

∧∧∧

Walter R. 1972. How Europe Underdeveloped Africa. 2009 Edition. Panaf publishing, Inc.
en.wikipedia.org/../developing country.
en.wikipedia.org/wiki/first world.
en.wikipidia.org/wiki/good governance.
en.wikipedia.org/wiki/Maslow's-hierarchy of needs.
en.wikipedia.org/wiki/ transfer of technology.
en.wikipedia.org/ wiki/ third-world.
www.answers.com/federal system of government.
www.lifehack.org/communication/
www.nationsonline.org/one world/thir....
www.autm.net/ tech-transfer.htm

THE AUTHOR
The author hails from Ogwoazu Okue, Ishiagu, Ivo Local Government Area of Ebonyi State. He campaigns for value re – orientation in developing nations of the world. Okorie Ndubuisi Simon is a minister of the word, a consultant and has authored several books for the benefit of mankind.

THE BOOK
I refer to your letter sent to the Nigerian Educational Research and Development

Council (NERDC) for the assessment of your book.

2.   The book has been assessed and found to be useful. It is therefore recommended.

3.   Please, accept the assurance of the Honourable Minister's highest regards

G.O. ODEWALE
For: Honourable Minister of Education
Federal Ministry of Education

This is to acknowledge receipt of your letter on the above subject matter dated 20/01/12 and to congratulate you for the book which we consider an important intellectual contribution to the discourse on Nigeria.

I am to assure you that the Agency shall be on hand to promote the sale and distribution of the book to as many Nigerians as possible.

Accept the Director General's warm regards and best wishes.

C. M. IKYOH
Director (Mass Mobilization)
For: Director General
National Orientation Agency

I am directed to acknowledge receipt of your letter dated 18th January, 2012 on the above subject and to congratulate you on the production of such a timely, germane and well researched work on attitudinal change against corruption.

^^^

2. The Commission would wish to purchase 20 copies of the book when a price is fixed
3. Please, accept the assurances of the Hon. Minister/Deputy Chairman's regards.
A. A. Taiwo
Assistant Director (Human Capital)
For: Hon Minister/Deputy Chairman
National Planning Commission

ᶺᶺᶺ